A HEAVENLY JOURNEY

A HEAVENLY JOURNEY

(A Fictional Story Based on Historical and Biblical Facts)

by
Veralyn R. Alpha

Published by
FAITH PUBLISHING COMPANY
P.O. BOX 237
MILFORD, OHIO 45150

Nihil Obstat: Reverend Ralph J. Lawrence
                January 17, 1994

The Nihil Obstat and Imprimatur are a declaration that a book or pamphlet is to be considered to be free from doctrinal or moral error. It is not implied that those who have granted the Nihil Obstat and Imprimtur agree with the contents, opinions or statements expressed.

Imprimatur: Most Reverend Carl K. Moeddel
                Auxiliary Bishop and Vicar General
                Archdiocese of Cincinnati
                January 24, 1994

Published by Faith Publishing Company
    P.O. Box 237
    Milford, Ohio 45150
    1-800-576-6477

Book dealers may acquire additional copies of this book by contacting the publisher.

Individuals may acquire additional copies through your local religious bookstore, or contact: The Riehle Foundation
                P.O. Box 7
                Milford, Ohio
                513-576-0032

Copyright © 1994 Veralyn R. Alpha

ISBN: 1-880033-15-1

Library of Congress Catalog Card No.: 94-072392

Printed in the United States

All rights reserved. No part of this book may be reproduced or transmitted in any form or by any means whatsoever without the written permission of the publisher.

Dedication

Dedicated to a loyal shepherd, Fr. Joe Benson, who lovingly agreed to assist me in the spiritual end of editing this book and who has been such an inspiration in my life.

V.R.A.

Table of Contents

Preface ix

Introduction xi

Chapter 1
(1994) 1

Chapter 2
(53 A.D.)   St. Paul, the Apostle 4

Chapter 3
(96 A.D.)   St. Clement of Rome 9

Chapter 4
(110 A.D.)   St. Ignatius of Antioch 16

Chapter 5
(150 A.D.)   St. Justin Martyr 23

Chapter 6
(156 A.D.)   St. Polycarp 32

Chapter 7
(160 A.D.)   Gravesite of St. Peter 35

Chapter 8
(180 A.D.)   St. Irenaeus 40

Chapter 9
(200 A.D.)   Baptismal Ceremony 47

Chaper 10
(383 A.D.)   St. Jerome 52

Chapter 11
(400 A.D.)   St. Augustine 62

Chapter 12
(1517)   Martin Luther—Reformation 70

Bibliography 83

Author's Preface

The premise of this account begins with a simple question to the reader: **"If it were possible for you to visit the early Church, would your beliefs be the same, or would the first Christians have considered you heretical or schismatic?"**

Although the story of Carter Roberts is fictitious, the information quoted and the words of the archangel Gabriel are based on historical and Biblical facts primarily gathered from unbiased sources such as encyclopedias, Bibles and other reference books. Because the story emphasizes the "factual" side, the fictional details are unimportant. The only objective was to encourage the reader to examine his or her beliefs and then compare them to the beliefs of the first Christians.

Catholic beliefs that existed in the early Church and addressed herein are the Eucharist, "Faith Alone" and Good Works, the Apocrypha, the "Bible Alone" and Sacred Tradition, Relics, Apostolic Succession, the Papacy, Confession, Infant Baptism, Purgatory, and lastly Mary, called the "New Eve" by Justin Martyr (100-165 A.D.).

Introduction

Father Joseph A. Benson

Many are the challenges, great are the obstacles but in each time and in each age, the Lord blessed us with that constant reminder. . ."My Spirit will lead you into all truth." That was very especially understood by the great Apologists of former times who were, I would say, raised up in their vocation as Christians to explain, defend, and aid toward defining the Faith of the people of God. Their calling arose in the very specific settings of their times, and threads of that calling very often were to be found in their own background stories. Thus, from their wealth, they were blessed to share and illumine, carefully illustrate and lovingly demonstrate the nature of the Truth that is ours to guard and defend and, in as many ways as possible, to share with the world.

And so into our day, we are blessed by sisters and brothers given that unique charism. I feel privileged to recommend this little "story" that is very clearly enlivened with such a charism. What makes it *appealing*, I would dare suggest, is the story-line style. What makes it *effective* is the patient research and orthodox grounding in terms of history and the teaching of some of the great Fathers of the Church. Veralyn has certainly done no small service to Catholics seeking material to better understand the basis of all that they believe and to be able to use in defense of their faith when they come in contact with sisters and brothers in the faith who sadly misrepresent Catholicism, or who have had such misrepresentations happen to them in the name of Gospel Truth and Biblical Fundamentals. The author invites the reader to enjoy, but also to ponder, and maybe even to begin the process of sharing, caring, and defining for the times that are ours, the Faith that is ours in Christ Jesus, through His Church.

> Father Joseph A. Benson
> St. Margaret Mary Church
> Slidell, LA

Chapter 1

1994

Carter Roberts was a young Protestant evangelist who carried the word of God, his Holy Bible, in his hand as if it were a sword. His congregation anxiously anticipated his spirited Sunday sermons. Routinely, he asked those he met, "Are you saved?" He often preached that Christians were saved through the "Bible Alone" and "Faith Alone" and that we could confess our sins only to God. Although he was an honorable man, in his faith, he truly believed that only adults could be baptized and that Catholics were going to Hell for their belief in the Real Presence of Christ in the Eucharist.

For Carter, this particular day had turned out to be heavily scheduled with church affairs. As he closed his Bible and reached for the lamp on his nightstand, he was anxious to retire for the evening. His body ached for a good night's rest, and he soon fell into a deep sleep.

In the middle of the night, Carter suddenly awoke to a blinding light that encompassed every corner of the room. Before him stood the archangel Gabriel, a towering figure, mighty and exuding heavenly authority. Carter *knew* it was Gabriel before he spoke one word of his heavenly message. His golden hair and pale skin seemed luminous, appearing to glow from within. The angel's words resounded as though they were almost an echo: "I am the archangel Gabriel. I have been sent by God to accompany you on a heavenly journey back to the time of the first Christians and the early Church! This will enable you to understand that your present beliefs might have been deemed 'heretical' by the first Christians! As a teacher of God's Holy Word, you must realize that you have fallen into beliefs that were never practiced before the Middle Ages. Through no fault of your own, you have never fully comprehended that there existed only one Church, one flock, one shepherd. Prepare to leave at once!"

Carter struggled to stand on his feet and reason with his sanity! The stillness of the moment and the heavenly being before him was overpowering and quite incomprehensible! He wondered, "Is this a dream?" At once, a knowledge that seemed to come from deep within erased that thought instantly and completely.

Trembling with excitement, he quickly assessed the way he was dressed and silently wondered if his nightly attire was appropriate for his journey. This reflection was no more in his mind when he noticed the angel seemingly reading his heart. Looking down once again, he discovered that he was dressed in simple apparel of what he assumed were Biblical times: a brown robe with a long cloth draped over his right shoulder. His waist was tied with a heavy cord and brown leather sandals were on his feet.

Gabriel glanced once again at Carter, who quickly snatched his Bible sitting on the nightstand. Seeing this, the angel produced several books and handed them to Carter saying: "I see you are bringing God's Holy Bible with you. This is pleasing to God! However, we will also bring along several encyclopedias which are completely unbiased references to help verify that your present beliefs are derived from biased sources, including anti-Catholic writers. It is these writings that have contributed to your unrelenting prejudice against the Catholic faith. Therefore, these references and several other publications will enable you to better understand that what you have interpreted to be God's Holy Word was never believed before in the history of the Church!

"Carter, you are asked to simply observe as we travel back through time to the early years of the Church. Our intention will not be one of confrontation, but education. Simply observe what the early Church believed so that you can contrast it to current beliefs."

As they began their journey, Gabriel announced that he wanted Carter to witness a momentous occasion, that of Carter's favorite apostle preaching to the early Christians from Holy Scripture. In an enveloping brilliance that seemed to appear almost instantaneously, they began their heavenly journey!

Chapter 2

53 A.D.

Carter could not believe his eyes, for there stood **Paul** the apostle that he so fervently quoted in almost every Sunday sermon. It was an early spring morning, and the crowd listened intently as he stood on a steep hillside proclaiming God's *Word* to the Romans. However, the scriptures from which he cited so eloquently were from the *Septuagint*, the Old Testament scriptures used by the early Christians. Gabriel motioned to Carter to be seated and said, "You can see that Paul is totally unaware that his words will one day be considered 'scripture' and that Christians will number his sentences and argue over them fifteen hundred years later." Gabriel instantly referred to the *Encyclopedia Britannica* as a further reference. It stated that in the **NEW TESTAMENT**, the earliest pieces of Christian literature to be collected seems to have been the letters of Paul, but it could appear that initially, at least, they did not qualify as *Scripture*.

Gabriel then advised Carter to refer to his own Bible and told him: "The scriptures from which Paul is quoting were contained in the Greek *Septuagint*, the Old Testament scriptures of the Greek-speaking Jews that was translated into Greek about 200 years before Christ. During the time of Christ and the apostles, both Old Testament scriptures (the Hebrew Jews of Palestine and the Greek Jews of Alexandria) were recognized as authoritative. However, it is from the *Septuagint*, the Greek Old Testament that Paul now quotes, for it was the Bible of the early Christians. What is even more significant is the fact that the *Septuagint* contained the seven books of the Bible that Martin Luther eliminated 1500 years later, the same books which you call the *Apocrypha* (*Tobit, Judith, Wisdom, Sirach, Baruch, 1* and *2 Maccabees*, the last six chapters of *Esther* and three passages of *Daniel* 3:24-90). Please keep in mind that the New Testament did not exist at this time. Now refer to the 'informational pages' of your Protestant King James version of the Bible, as well as the Revised Standard Version to verify what I have just revealed to you."

Carter opened his King James Version Bible and incredulously read that it reported that the early Christians, including Paul, used the Old Testament *Septuagint* which contained the *Apocrypha*. It stated:

> **Septuagint:** "Besides all the books of the Hebrew Bible, it also contained several small books, now called *The Apocrypha*... In the time of our Lord, it was generally used and quoted by New Testament writers, especially by Paul." (*King James Version Bible, School and Library Reference Edition*)
>
> The Revised Standard Version Bible stated: "It was only natural that it [LXX-*Septuagint*] became the Old Testament which was read in the early Christian churches. And too, it was natural for the authors of the Old Testament books to use the LXX when they wished to quote the Old Testament."

Gabriel went on to point out, "Catholics refer to these same seven Books that are missing from your Bible as *Deuterocanonical*, meaning that they were definitely accepted into the canon as inspired, but only after some debate. The word *Apocrypha* means something entirely different to a Catholic, for it refers to those writings lacking canonicity that are from a completely different larger group of books that were never accepted by any council as inspired, such as the apocryphal book, the *Gospel of Thomas*. However, when writing the New Testament, the authors indeed referred to these other seven books commonly called the *Apocrypha* by Protestants."

Looking for additional verification, Carter turned to the

Encyclopedia Britannica. He read: "Among the books to which the New Testament refers are several of the *Deuterocanonical* books of the Old Testament [*Apocrypha*], as well as some books, such as *Enoch*, that do not belong to any canon...For most of the early Christian Fathers, the Old Testament meant the *Septuagint,* since few of them other than Origen knew Hebrew." (*Encyclopedia Britannica*)

Checking a further non-religious source, The *Encyclopedia Americana,* Carter read: "The LXX [*Septuagint*] is the original of most of the ancient versions of the Old Testament... Of 350 direct Old Testament quotations in the New Testament, scarcely 50 disagree materially with the LXX."

Gabriel then informed Carter that the early Fathers quoted from these books and regarded them as scripture: "Even the catechumens were being taught from books of the *Apocrypha*..."

> "Clement of Alexandria, Origen and Cyprian not only quoted passages in the *Apocrypha,* but they specifically regarded them as scripture. Athanasius reports that catechumens were taught part of the *Apocrypha,* which he freely cites as scripture. The same point of view prevails in Chrysostom, Ambrose, Augustine, and other church fathers."
> (*The Interpreter's Bible*)

As he read these simple facts, Gabriel noticed that Carter appeared a little shaken because these facts were never known to him before. Allowing him to regain his composure, Gabriel continued: "There were no 'Bible Christians' in the early Church because in reality, there was no Bible which contained the Old and New Testament with the official canon, as you know it, for the first four hundred years. Yet Christians were still being saved! 'Scripture' to the early Christians meant the *Septuagint,* the Old Testament scriptures which referred to these Deuterocanonical books and were used by the early Christians because they followed 'Apostolic tradition' rather than the synagogue."

Gabriel further pointed out that the encyclopedias they had brought with them also verified that the early Christian Church, which claimed to follow tradition rather than the rules of the synagogue raised no question about the sanctity of any of the books found in the Greek collection believed to have been used by the Apostles.

"The inclusion of the Apocrypha in the Septuagint has caused some scholars to conclude that there were two Jewish canons, a narrower one current in Palestine and a broader one current in the Greek-speaking world. Most scholars, however, have drawn the inference that the Jewish collection of sacred books was still in a *fluid* state in the 2nd century B.C., that the status of the Apocrypha as well as that of some books in the Hagiographa was unclear. This circumstance permitted these books to be included in the Septuagint." (*Encyclopedia Britannica*)

Knowing this was contrary to what the evangelist had always held to be true, Gabriel continued: "Thus, the Bible as you know it with a fixed canon of 'inspired' Books did not exist for almost four hundred years, but when the canon was firmed up, it included the Deuterocanonical books of the so-called *Apocrypha*. Why? Although most of the New Testament books were acknowledged as being 'inspired' as early as the 2nd century, it was not until the 4th century that a 'universal' list of books existed. Prior to that time, there were disagreements over which books were to be included in the official canon of the Bible. In 382 A.D., Pope Damasus commissioned Jerome to interpret the various existing Latin translations. At first, Jerome distinguished several books by comments in the prefaces of his Latin *Vulgate*, but Augustine provided a catalog of Old Testament books that also included the books that you call the *Apocrypha*. Under the guidance of the Holy Spirit, this catalog was officially confirmed in 393 A.D. at the Council of Hippo, at the Council of Carthage in 397 A.D. and 419 A.D., and by Pope Innocent I in 405 A.D. After the Reformation, it was reconfirmed at the Council of Trent in 1545."

Carter and his new-found angel friend poured over additional reference material to substantiate Gabriel's claims.

"Prior to the end of the fourth century, however, there was controversy over the inspired character of several works—the *Letter of the Hebrews, James, Jude, 2 Peter, 2* and *3 John,* and *Revelation.* Controversy ended in the fourth century and these books, along with those about which there was no dispute were enumerated in the canon stated by the Councils of Hippo and Carthage and affirmed by Innocent I in 405." (1992 *Catholic Almanac*)

CANON (4th century): "No universally acknowledged list existed, though the African churches, for example, in the 4th century expressly recognized a canon identical with that later found in the *Vulgate* (therefore, including the *Apocrypha*), and this was approved by the Bishop of Rome to whom they submitted it." (*Encyclopedia Americana*)

Encouraging this line of reasoning, Gabriel also clarified that many of the *Dead Sea Scrolls* lean heavily toward the use of the *Septuagint,* including the books of *Tobit* and *Sirach*, which were not included in the Protestant Bible. He again suggested Carter verify it through a check in the reference books.

DEAD SEA SCROLLS: "Some of the manuscripts present a text related closely to that of the *Septuagint,* the ancient Greek translation that was the Old Testament of the early Christian Church... Several of the books previously known as the *Apocrypha* and *Pseudepigrapha* appear among the Qumran texts. They include *Tobit* and *Sirach* (*Ecclesiasticus*)..." (*Encyclopedia Britannica*)

Though not convinced, Carter made a mental note to read the seven books missing from his Protestant Bible as soon as he was returned home. Perhaps there was something he had been missing. "Wait," Gabriel said, reading Carter's thoughts; "there is much more for you to discover."

Chapter 3

96 A.D.

There was that blinding flood of light again, and Carter suddenly found himself in a rather spacious room that seemed to be a open porch or a type of breezeway with towering pillars and a marble floor. Though they were still in Rome, Gabriel quickly informed him that he was in the presence of one of the oldest of the Apostolic Fathers, **Clement of Rome,** author of *I, Clement* (*Letter of the Corinthians*) and fourth in line to the papacy, the "chair of Peter" as it was later called.

Seated at an elongated table, St. Clement appeared to be totally preoccupied in his writing and completely unaware of their presence. Gabriel then proudly proclaimed: "Many of the early Church leaders declared that Clement was a pope, consecrated by Peter himself, and the same Clement spoken of in the New Testament in the Book of *Philippians.* There was only one Church, and Clement wrote on the critical importance of keeping it ONE through Apostolic Succession and spoke in the name of the Roman Church. Encyclopedias are not end-all answers in matters of faith, Carter, but let's just see what they say about Clement."

St. Clement I: "pope from 88 to 97 or from 92 to 101, according to Tertullian was consecrated by St. Peter. Irenaeus lists him as a third successor of Peter, contemporary of the Apostles and witness of their preaching... Origen, Epiphanius, Eusebius and Jerome identify him with the Clement of

Philippians iv., 3." (*Encyclopedia Britannica,* "Clement")

"Clement of Rome speaks in the name of the Roman Church and insisting upon the importance of apostolic succession of presbyters (not altogether differentiated from bishops), gives instructions to the church at Corinth." (*Encyclopedia Britannica,* "Apostolic Fathers")

As he handed the evangelist an encyclopedia, Gabriel wanted to emphasize the critical relevance of a significant fact of history and revealed, "It is also imperative for you to note that Clement speaks of the necessity to do 'good works' in his historical writing, *I, Clement.* Yes Carter, before the end of this century, before the Church was even 70 years old, the importance of 'good works' was duly stressed. There was never a 'faith alone' doctrine until the Reformation because this was strictly a personal enlightenment of Martin Luther."

Opening an encyclopedia to assist in his complete understanding of the magnitude of this influential Apostolic Father's role in the history of the Church, Carter read the following words in amazement:

Towards the end of the 1st century, Clement "wrote in the name of the Roman Church to the Church of Corinth, in order to urge its dissident members to return to peace and apostolic order. His letters were regarded as *scripture* by many Christians of the 3rd and 4th centuries, and by some even later. The principal subjects discussed in *I, Clement* are as follows: (1) the troubles at Corinth... (2) the need for repentance... (3) the importance of resurrection... (4) the necessity of good works... (5) the apostolic succession... (6) need for reconciliation and love... (7) need for humility and obedience... (8) need to pray (9) summary..." (*Encyclopedia Britannica, "Apostolic Fathers"*)

96 A.D.

Gabriel persevered: "Unfortunately Carter, you must realize that after 1,500 years, it was Martin Luther who personally interpreted the words of Paul in *Romans* 3:28. Although St. Peter warned Christians to be found without spot or blemish, he also warned them in *2 Peter* 3:14-18, that the words of Paul were 'hard' to understand:"

"...So our beloved brother Paul wrote to you according to the wisdom given him, speaking of this as he does in all his letters. There are some things in them hard to understand, which the ignorant and unstable twist to their own destruction, as they do the other scriptures. You therefore, beloved, knowing this beforehand, beware lest you be carried away with the error of lawless men and lose your own stability." (*2 Peter* 3:14-18)

Expressing his sorrow with a deep sigh, Gabriel offered: "In his own German translation of the Bible, it was Luther who added the word 'alone' to Paul's actual words of *Romans* 3:28 because he felt it was needed. Cast your eyes upon this startling report to verify the words I have just spoken. Even a secular book, the encyclopedia, attests to this misinterpretation."

"In his translation of the Bible, Luther came to add 'alone' after the word 'faith' in the verse, *'for we hold that a man is justified by faith apart from works of the law'* (*Roman* 3:28), because he felt it to be demanded by the German language." (*Encyclopedia Britannica*)

The Angel then proceeded with his own explanation of the one small verse that took on an entirely new meaning after 1500 years of Church history. It still stands as a source of division among Christians today. He said, "The Apostle Paul was only speaking of 'works of the law,' such as circumcision. If you would have only read the previous chapter of the same Book, *Romans* 2:6, you would have realized that God indeed judges us *'according to our works.'* If you had only continued reading the verses before and after *Romans* 3:28, you would have understood the context of the verse. You would also have achieved the complete understanding that 'works of the law' such as circumcision and 'good works' are two entirely different things. I can sense that you are disturbed by this discovery!"

"Disturbed? You bet I am," Carter said to himself. "Nor do I see a need to rely on the words of an encyclopedia over the words of God in the Bible."

To enable Carter to further comprehend the complete sadness of Luther's enlightenment of "faith alone," Gabriel then added, "Unfortunately, I must also disclose to you that Luther despised Moses because he thought that Moses insisted too strongly on the Law and its observances."

Still, Carter was beginning to perceive a certain truth in what the angel had declared. Gabriel stressed that in reality, the new doctrine of "faith alone" never existed because "good works" were absolutely necessary in the early Church and were rightly considered the "fruit" of the faith.

Previously, their presence on the far side of the room had gone unnoticed by St. Clement, who seemed preoccupied with his writing. Now, he anxiously glanced their way, but his puzzled expression soon disappeared as the angel justified his unique mission to the Apostolic Father. With a sense of relief, Clement nodded and readily commenced transcribing his notes.

"Where is Clement's Bible?" Carter asked. Gabriel sadly looked at him because he had not yet been able to fully comprehend all the angel had just revealed to him. Gabriel gently spoke to him, almost in a whisper: "Carter, history has recorded that the Church existed 'before' the Bible. The Bible as you know it comes from...the Church, the Catholic Church...the same church that you won't recognize. Though the Old Testament, most of the Gospels, and many other books and writings such as St. Clement's were in existence, it had not yet been decided which books were inspired to form the canon of the Bible. And yet, Christians were still being saved! Stressing this point, Gabriel's voice grew stronger. "Just as the theory of 'faith alone' did not exist in the early Church, neither did the theory of the 'BIBLE ALONE' exist, because the New Testament was not assembled until the fourth century! Yes, Christians were being saved through Faith, but it was also Sacred Tradition, the early writings of the Fathers and Doctors of the Church, AND Scripture that guided them.

You often quote Paul as an advocate of the Bible Alone theory when you cite *2 Timothy* 3:15-17: *'All scripture is inspired by God and is useful for teaching, for regulation, for correction and for training in righteousness so that one who belongs to God may be competent, equipped for every good work.'* However, as you will plainly see by referring to the Britannica, these particular verses merely allude to the scriptures of Timothy's boyhood, the Old Testament! If anything, by quoting these verses to uphold the Bible alone theory, you would simply establish the fact that the New Testament is not necessary for your salvation. Consider all that I have just related to you..."

"Christians usually have to think twice to realize that there was once a time when the Christian Bible did not contain both the Old *and* New Testament. New Testament statements such as *2 Timothy* 3:16, 'All scripture is inspired by God,' are predicated on what came later to be called the Old Testament; so are many of the references to 'Scripture' in the early Fathers. Only gradually, did Christians find it *necessary* to add a second collection of sacred books as the 'New' Testament alongside the Old... The task of sifting through the writings of the early church and of identifying this apostolic witness occupied Christians well into the 4th century."
(*Encyclopedia Britannica*, "Bible")

Gabriel concluded his explanation by firmly stating: "To continue on this journey, you must understand the importance of Sacred Tradition and the writings of the Apostolic Fathers such as Clement. 'Unity' was preserved throught the interpretation of Sacred Scripture through the teachings of the Apostolic Fathers, Fathers and Doctors of the early Church, not individuals such as yourself! Beliefs today should coincide with those of the first Christians, because those who ignored the 'Tradition' of the Apostolic Fathers were considered heretics and schismatics!"

Opening the Britannica, the archangel said, "Notice that the following information clearly indicates that early Fathers appealed not to the Bible, but to an historical writing called the 'rule of faith.' Why? Because the Bible as you know it did not exist as yet. Therefore, Sacred Tradition and Sacred Scripture were considered 'parallel norms' as early as the second century..."

> "It was in the **2nd century**, however, that the church became increasingly aware of the need for keeping its teaching uncontaminated and devising criteria for testing deviations. The Apostolic Fathers (q.v.) appealed to 'the prophets and apostles' and Irenaeus and Tertullian laid great stress on the *rule of faith,* a loose summary of essential articles handed down from apostolic times. About this time, Scripture and tradition were recognized as parallel norms enshrining the same truths."
> (*Encyclopedia Britannica,* "Heresy")

Carter's head was spinning! Although this messenger of God had somewhat opened his heart, his mind remained blocked with a myriad of memorized Bible verses that persevered unrelentlessly in fast procession through his intellect. Certainly, he did not want to argue with an archangel, who as a heavenly messenger of God could only bring forth His true Word. Realizing that Gabriel had only brought along the reference books to demonstrate to Carter that simple historical facts are recorded and can be found with little effort, the initial reaction of the evangelist to these alarming truths was greatly conflicting. He struggled to find the precise words to boldly assert his reasons for his beliefs to the Bible Alone theory. Yet, it was as if a great battle seemed to be taking place in his mind between what he had always believed to be true and now what was indeed truth, delivered to him by a messenger of God. Yet, first and foremost, the nature of his character was an inborn temperament of true *obedience*, reserving a great deal of parental respect and for other authoritative individuals who were influential throughout his life. However, as an adult, pleasing God was the significant and fundamental priority in Carter's life now. This kept his heart open, as his earnest desire was only to genuinely recognize and attain truth.

"Why didn't I search for myself?" he thought. "How could Christians be saved by the Bible Alone, when the *New Testament* did not evolve until the 4th century?" The importance of Sacred Tradition and the fact that Christians were still being "saved" during this period had simply never occurred to him! This penetrating realization of his failure to ever search for the truth became more clear as the interior battle seemed to subside.

As suddenly as they had arrived, the two of them were then swept away to another time. The journey was just beginning, and Carter had much to learn from this heavenly messenger.

Chapter 4

110 A.D.

Carter found himself on a lonely road just outside the amphitheater in Rome. Gabriel informed his companion that another Apostlic Father of the Church, **Ignatius,** Bishop of Antioch, was on his way to martyrdom by being thrown to the lions. "Carter, Ignatius had a great hatred of heresy and schism and a compelling, passionate desire for the unity of the Church. He wrote seven authentic letters to the Christians of the early Church that are a part of Church history. According to the *Encyclopedia Britannica*, as early as the 2nd century, the name 'Catholic Church,' was used to distinguish the church at large from heretical sects because in **110** A.D., it is recorded that Ignatius once said, **'Wherever the Bishop is, there let the people be, as where Jesus is, there is the Catholic Church.'** My friend, where is the bishop of your church?

"The encyclopedia defines 'Catholic' as derived from a Greek word meaning 'universal' and used by ecclesiastical writers since the 2nd century to distinguish the church at large from local communities or *heretical* and schematic sects."

Gabriel hastily informed the young preacher that Ignatius was a disciple of the Apostles themselves and well-known in Church history. Fighting for the unity of beliefs, he was vehement in his historical confrontation with the heretical Docetists who denied the reality of the humanity of Christ.

Opening the *Enyclopedia of Early Christianity,* Gabriel's finger moved across the following words to prove to Carter that Ignatius was unyielding in his fight for the belief in the Real Presence of Christ in the Eucharist.

ST. IGNATIUS OF ANTIOCH

"I have no delight in corruptible food, nor in the pleasures of this life. I desire the bread of God, the heavenly bread, the bread of life, which is the flesh of Jesus Christ, the Son of God, who became afterwards of the seed of David and Abraham; and I desire the drink of God, namely His blood, which is incorruptible love and eternal life."

(Ignatius, 110 A.D., *Letter to the Romans*)

"Realist language about the eucharist occurs in the second century mainly to counter Docetic and Gnostic ideas that denied to Christ a real physical body. Ignatius referred to those who avoided the eucharist because of its association with the flesh of Christ." (*Encyclopedia of Christianity*, "Real Presence")

"They [Docetists] abstain from the Eucharist and prayer because they do not confess that the Eucharist is the Flesh of Our Savior Jesus Christ, which suffered for our sins, and which the Father, in His goodness raised up again." (Igantius, 110 A.D., *Letter to the Smyrneans*)

"Look to the early Church for what was believed by the first Christians," Gabriel wisely cautioned. "The *Didache*, an important document of the early Church believed to have been written toward the end of the 1st or 2nd century, reflected the liturgy and beliefs of the first Christians. They believed that only the baptized Christian could share in the Eucharist and the *Didache* 9 understood Jesus' words, '*Give not that which is holy to the dogs*' (*Matthew* 7:6), as applying to the Eucharist. This is confirmed, once again, in this *Encyclopedia of Early Christianity*."

Carter noticed the smile on the face of St. Ignatius as he bravely marched to his death. As Ignatius passed Gabriel and Carter, he looked deeply into their eyes. Gabriel then opened the Bible to *John* 6:28-71 and read aloud the passage beginning with the crowd who had just witnessed Jesus perform two miracles. Yet, this same crowd still demanded another *sign* in verse 30 and challenged Him to produce a third miracle compared to the heavenly manna sent to Moses.

The angel began to speak: "It is imperative that you read all of the verses of *John* 6 in order that you fully understand why Ignatius was so very willing to suffer martyrdom for this 'Bread' of Christ that the prophet Malachi foretold was to come as a pure offering, and which St. Jerome translated as a 'clean oblation' in *Malachi* 1:11. Notice, my friend, that although the Lord answered the crowd's request for a 'sign' by promising them His own 'Living Bread' that He would give them always, they still murmured and walked away from Him! If His words, *Unless you eat my Body and drink my Blood* were only metaphorical, this would not have been difficult for the assembled crowd to believe! After all, they had just witnessed Our Lord produce two miracles in *John* 6—the feeding of the 5,000, and His walking on the water. Yet, they stayed with Him, asking for a third sign! But to accept His answer that this 'sign' that He would give was truly His Body and Blood...this they could not tolerate. The Biblical word 'sign' clearly meant 'miracle'..."

Opening the Bible to *John* 6, Gabriel promptly announced that the Greek words in verse 54 should have been correctly translated *to chew* rather than simply *to eat* His flesh: "Carter, the crowds that challenged Jesus for a miracle left Him because they could not believe Him! Jesus knew that not all would believe His words! Read verse 64 for Jesus said, *And there are some of you that do not believe!* There must have been something to believe! The Lord makes it clear that His words were not figurative! Christians of your time can learn much by reading *Psalms* 78 because just as the crowd in the Old Testament also challenged God and received many miracles, including the raining down of manna, they too still sinned and believed not! The belief in the Real Presence of Our Lord in the Eucharist has existed for 2,000 years. Even Luther and many of the Reformers believed in the Real Presence. In fact, approximately 75 percent of the world's Christians, including Catholic, Orthodox, Anglicans, Episcopals and Lutherans teach the belief in the Real Presence based on the words of Christ in *John* 6. Yet, in your country this percentage plunges because of the many Protestant sects."

It was enough to invoke a response. Pondering all the angel had said, Carter suddenly spoke aloud to Gabriel, "Why did I not understand the crucial words of *John* 6, His *Living Bread?* Why did I take the Bible verses so literally, and yet ignore the very words of Our Lord?"

Gabriel peered at Carter and gently responded, "The

answer is that the Lord said in *Mark* 10:15. *Truly I say to you, whoever does not receive the kingdom of God like a child, shall not enter it!* How could the bread that He would give only 'represent' His body if the Lord proclaimed that it was His 'Living' Bread? Just as He further explained being 'reborn' in baptism to Nicodemus using the words 'water and spirit' in *John* 3, the Lord also warned three chapters later in *John* 6: *It is the spirit that gives life, the flesh is of no avail; the words that I have spoken to you are spirit and life.* Thus, it is the word, the prayers of the consecration that gives us His 'living' bread, just as the word gives us the 'living' water of Baptism! This was not a parable! The crowd that had followed Him asked for a third miracle! The word they used for miracle was 'sign.' Therefore, Jesus did not say, 'My Body is "like" the Bread of Heaven...' Emphatically, He stated: *For my flesh IS food indeed...* Yet, they responded, *This is a hard saying* and murmured among themselves. His response was, *Do you take offense at this?* For the Lord was indeed delivering to them the third miracle! However, this time it was to be the ultimate test of their faith! Carter, why do you believe that Jesus could heal the sick, turn water into wine, raise the dead and walk on water? Yet, when He gave you the words of eternal life, you also walked away! The explanation is that the crowd could not SEE this miracle, for it required great faith! Blessed are they that do not see and yet believe! Belief in the Eucharist is 'True' faith, the greatest Faith of all!"

> *For this reason, they could not believe, because again Isaiah said: "He blinded their eyes and hardened their heart, so that they might not see with their eyes and understand with their heart and be converted, and I will heal them."* (*John* 12:39-40).

"Carter, in 350 A.D., St. Cyril of Jerusalem explained in his 'Catechetical Lectures,' that after the invocation of the Holy Spirit, the bread was no longer simple bread, but the Body of Christ. In the same lectures, he also cautioned those who were about to receive Holy Communion to 'make of your left hand a throne for the right, since you are about to receive into it a King.' Lecturing the communicant to be careful with 'what is more precious than gold and gems,' he also warned that not a particle of the Body of Christ may escape."

Looking towards Heaven, Carter silently prayed, "Lord, forgive me...if by ridiculing your very own words, I have been no better than those that mocked and scourged you when they crowned you King of the Jews... Still, Lord, I am not convinced that reference books and the words of these so-called 'Saints' have any priority over my own many years of studying Your Scriptures."

Gabriel smiled at his guest and explained that they must be on their way once again for he wanted Carter to witness a typical Mass of 150 A.D. to further demonstrate the importance of belief of the Real Presence in the Eucharist.

ST. JUSTIN MARTYR

"For it is not as common bread nor common drink that we recieve these, but as by God's word, Jesus Christ Our Savior became flesh and blood for our salvation, so also we have been taught that the food made Eucharist by the word of prayer that comes from Him is both Flesh and Blood of that Jesus who was made flesh."

(Justin Martyr, *First Apology*, 150 A.D.)

Chapter 5

150 A.D.

Almost instantly, Carter discovered that they were present at a Mass in Rome in the year 150 A.D. Gabriel explained that the powerful man speaking in the front of the room was **Justin Martyr**, another important historical figure in early Church history who had opened a school of Christian philosophy in Rome. An early Father and great apologist, Justin called Mary the *New Eve* in his work, *Dialogue with Trypho* and also recorded for us, in his *First Apology*, an historical description of an early Mass.

The mighty angel confided, "Listen as Justin explains to the crowd why they now gather to worship on Sunday, the day after that of Kronos. Keep in mind that when the Pharisees criticized the disciples for picking grain on the Sabbath, Jesus said, *For the Son of Man is Lord of the Sabbath.*" (*Matthew* 12:8).

> "The Day of the Sun is the day on which we all gather in a common meeting, because it is the first day on which God, changing darkness and matter, created the world; and it is the day on which Jesus Christ Our Savior rose from the dead. For He was crucified on the day before that of Kronos [Saturday]; and on the day after that of Kronos, which is the day of the Sun, having appeared to His apostles and disciples, He taught them these things, which we have submitted to you also for your consideration." (Justin Martyr, *First Apology*, 150 A.D.)

Carter was relieved that the faith he practiced did indeed worship on Sunday; however, the angel interrupted his thoughts and spoke with authority. "Now pay close attention to the words of Justin as he explains the Eucharist, by stating that it is not lawful for anyone to participate unless they have been baptized unto a 'new birth' and believe the teaching to be true."

> "And this food is with us called Eucharist, and it is not lawful for any man to partake of it but him who believes our teaching to be true, and has been washed with the washing which is for the forgiveness of sins, and unto a new birth, and lives as Christ commanded. For it is **not** as common bread or common drink that we receive these, but as by God's word, Jesus Christ Our Savior became flesh and blood for our salvation. So also we have been taught that the food made Eucharist by the word of prayer that comes from Him is both Flesh and Blood of that Jesus who was made flesh. For the Apostles in the memoirs which they composed, which are called Gospels, have thus recorded that they were given command—that Jesus took bread and gave thanks and said, *Do this in remembrance of Me; this is My Body;* and took the cup likewise and gave thanks and said, *This is My Blood,* and gave of it only to them..." *(First Apology)*

Looking at his traveling companion with great compassion, Gabriel sorrowfully announced, "My friend, you see that you cannot partake of the Eucharist in this Mass because you have not believed this teaching to be true. Scripture points to the power of the Eucharist. The communion bread which you teach only 'represents' the Body of Christ! Read *Acts* 27:21-27, and you will see that though Paul and the other prisoners on the ship were starving, Paul assured them that an angel had appeared and announced that all would be saved! After Paul blessed and broke the bread and gave it to them, they threw the remaining wheat overboard! Eventually, all were indeed saved! *Luke* 24:13-31 also tells of two men who met Jesus after His resurrection on the road to Emmaus, yet they did not recognize Him! They invited Him to stay with them. Only after He broke bread, blessed it and gave it to them were their eyes opened and they then recognized Him!''

Listening intently to every word, the young preacher inquired with great suspicion, ''What did Justin mean when he used the words 'new birth' in his explanation? Doesn't this mean they were born again?'' Peering straight into Carter's eyes, Gabriel responded, ''You can see that as early as 150 A.D., these first Christians understood the term 'new birth' or 'born again' to mean 'water baptism,' not a religious conversion experience of accepting Christ into one's life. It was the first step in God's plan of salvation. More importantly, one could not partake of the Eucharist unless they had been baptized with water and 'believed the teaching to be true.' *Acts* 10:44-48 clearly explains the difference between baptism of the Holy Spirit and the necessity of water baptism.''

Carter then noticed the people publicly **confessing** their sins before the bishop and the entire congregation that had assembled. As a Protestant, Carter only confessed his sins directly to God and expressly stated as much to the Angel. Gabriel explained in detail: ''Carter, you have always quoted *Matthew* 9:6 to show that only Jesus has the authority to forgive sins. However, the verse you have excluded is critical! Read *John* 20:21-23 and you will discover that as Our Lord prepared to leave the earth and His beloved apostles, He breathed on them the breath of the Holy Spirit and bestowed upon 'them' only His authority and power to 'bind and loose' sins saying, *Receive the Holy Spirit. If you forgive the sins of any, they are forgiven; if you retain the sins of any, they are retained.* Please note that this power was not given to the crowd on the mountain, and it specifically justifies the term 'Apostolic Succession' and the unbroken lineage of the Catholic Church that can easily be traced throughout history.

''Carter, Holy Scripture also tells us that the Priesthood was for those called. We are warned that one cannot confer this honor upon themselves! *Hebrews* 5:1-9 reads: *For every high priest chosen from among men is appointed to act on behalf of men in relation to God, to offer gifts and sacrifices for sins...And one does not take the honor upon himself, but he is called by God, just as Aaron was...you are a priest forever in the order of Melchizedek.* Therefore, the bishop or priest has the power to bind and loose sins, but they are His agent, His representative and ultimately, it is God who forgives the sinner. Note that Paul actually said...*All this is from God, who through Christ reconciled us to himself and gave us the ministry of reconciliation; that is, in Christ, God was reconciling the world to Himself, not counting their trespasses against them, and entrusting to us the message of reconciliation. So we are ambassadors for Christ, God making His appeal through us.* (*2 Corinthians* 5:18-19). Refer also to *1 Corinthians* 4:1; *John* 15:16. Carter, determine if even an encyclopedia attests to these truths!"

"In any event, a detailed *confession* of sins to the bishop or the priest appears quite early in the church's discipline of penance...In the early 3rd century, this discipline was called exomologesis ('confession'). Thereafter, the discipline was known in the east and west as penance. The discipline for the first five centuries was not everywhere uniform, but it followed a general pattern that reflects the action of St. Paul in delivering a serious offender over to Satan, 'for the destruction of the flesh,' and later in pardoning him or a similar offender lest he be 'overwhelmed by excessive sorrow' (*1 Corinthians* 5:5, *2 Corinthians* 2:7). Accordingly, there were two stages in the discipline of penance; excommunication, an exercise of the power of binding; and reconciliation, an exercise of the power of loosing. That this power affected the sinner's relations with God and not merely with the church is suggested by Christ's commission: 'whatever you bind on earth shall be bound in Heaven, and whatever you loose on earth, shall be loosed in Heaven' " (*Matthew* 18:18). (*Encyclopedia Britannica*)

"While we are on this subject of the priesthood, you have preached against the use of the word *Father* when referring to the priesthood. Paul called Timothy his son twice, in *Philippians* 2:22, and *1 Timothy* 1:2. In *1 Corinthians* 4:15, Paul called himself a 'father' when he said, *For though you have countless guides in Christ, you do not have many fathers. For I became your father in Christ Jesus through the gospel.* Carter, do not take the Bible so literally! What do you call the man married to your mother? Even the encyclopedias identify Clement, Ignatius, Justin, Irenaeus and many others as Fathers of the Church."

Opening the *Encyclopedia of Early Christianity*, the archangel wanted to elaborate on the history of Church organization, which was legislated sometime before the year 300 A.D. by the historical *Apostolic Church Order*, which is also called *Ecclesiastical Canons of the Holy Apostles*. It contained information from the *Didache* [70-140 A.D.].

> "Compiled from earlier sources, probably in Egypt ca. 300, the *Apostolic Church Order* gives ordinances ascribed individually to the twelve apostles (in a peculiar order), which they delivered in the presence of Martha and Mary. After an introduction (1-3), the first part (4-14) contains moral instructions similar to 'the two ways' found in the *Didache* and other early Christian literature. The second part (15-30) legislates on church organization, providing for a bishop, presbyters, reader, deacons, and widows and *excluding* women from the ministry of sacrificing the body and blood. Originally in Greek, the work also survives in Latin, Syriac, Copic, Arabic, and Ethiopic." (*Encyclopedia of Early Christianity*)

In greater detail, Gabriel affirmed another important belief. "**Celibacy** was valued by Jesus and Paul (*Matthew* 19:11-12; *1 Corinthians* 7:8; 20-35, and *Matthew* 19:27-30). There was no law that enforced celibacy during the first three centuries. It was only a matter of ecclesiastical discipline. However, in the west, the council of Elvira in Spain (c. 306) decreed that, 'it be entirely forbidden bishops, priests, deacons and all clergy placed in the ministry to live with their wives and beget sons. Whoever does this, let him be deprived of the distinction of the clergy.' A decretal of Pope Siricius in 386 ordered celibacy for 'priests and levites.' This decree was renewed by Innocent I (pope 401-417), and at the beginning of the 5th century, Leo I (*Epistle* 14) explained it so as to include subdeacons explicitly. This law has remained in force ever since, though during the early middle ages it was violated frequently. St. Boniface, St. Chrodegang of Metz, and Charlemagne did what they could to revive its observance and enforcement of celibacy was one of the principal aims of the reform of the clergy under St. Gregory VII (pope 1073-85)... The early Protestants rejected obligatory celibacy as something beyond any human power to impose, as contrary to the practice of the early church and as a source of scandal." Handing the *Encyclopedia Britannica* to Carter, to an already opened page, the Angel asked him to read. The words Carter read were exactly what he had just heard.

The young evangelist was overwhelmed by all he had just witnessed and read both in scripture and in the encyclopedias. Had he not been presented these truths by a messenger from Heaven, he would normally quote scriptures to debate with great fervor for the verification of his beliefs. Still, the Bible and faith alone—"that is where it is all at," he stated emphatically. "Isn't it?"

Gabriel attempted to ease his anxiety but explained that this was the purpose of his heavenly mission. "Carter, now that your heart has been opened to uncover truth, you must realize that through various recent interpretations and translations, Christians seemed to selectively embrace what they wanted to believe without consulting the early Fathers and Sacred Tradition. The Church is universal and 'Catholic' in belief for almost 2,000 years because of the fight against heresy, and the authority of the papacy against these other beliefs. The interpretation of God's Holy Words must not be for the individual to pick and choose Bible verses, decide what they mean, and then spread errors by preaching an out-of-context verse to an entire congregation. Here is where confusion and disorder evolves because when a Christian disagrees with what you have preached, they simply establish their own denomination. This was the result of the Reformation, the constant development of new Christian denominations with every new personal interpretation of Scripture. The ecclesiastical authority looks to the early Fathers for Bible interpretation, and all must come in agreement to preserve the unity Christ so desired."

> "The very heterogeneity of the Apostolic Fathers, in the form and content of their writings provides a valuable indication of the condition of Christianity immediately after, and to some extent contemporary *with* the writing of the New Testament. They show how the Pauline epistles were being *interpreted* (I Clement, Ignatius, Polycarp); the earlier ones seem to reflect a time when the sayings of Jesus, *not written gospels containing them,* were regarded as *authoritative,* though it is not always certain that written gospels were not being used. They reflect the development of ecclesiastical *authority*." (*Encyclopedia Britannica*)

"You state that the 'early Fathers,' as you call them, interpreted the Scriptures. Why should I accept their beliefs instead of what I interpret the meanings to be?" Carter asked.

Gabriel responded with great authority. "Again, you can see that the Catholic Church decides the interpretation of Scripture based on the Sacred Tradition of the early Fathers and thus, the unity of faith is preserved. Hence, it is both Sacred Tradition and Sacred Scripture that are important! All are to believe the same regarding the basic beliefs such as the Eucharist, Baptism, Confession, the Priesthood, and Mary."

Resuming along this line of thought, Gabriel expressed deep concern. "Carter, remember when Phillip asked the Ethiopian in *Acts* 8:30-31 if he understood the scripture he was reading in the Old Testament? His reply was, 'How can I unless someone guides me?' It was not until the Reformation that Luther decided that *everyone* could interpret the scriptures, and later regretted this decision because even though the Church had split into the East and West several hundred years before, the Christian world was still unified in basic Catholic beliefs. For fifteen hundred years, the basic beliefs were constant, but after the Reformation, the Church immediately began splitting into hundreds of different beliefs, all because of individual Bible interpretation! Which one is right? Christians began picking and choosing beliefs of the various reformers that agreed with their own individual interpretations, rather than following the Papacy and teachings of the early Fathers of the Church. To prevent turmoil and perserve unity, every country and every organization has a leader, creeds and/or by-laws they must follow. When the leadership is denied or replaced by rebelliousness, confusion results in the disobedience."

With his eyes downcast, Carter reflected on all the angel had just shown him. The thought that he could not worship with the first Christians was somehow devastating to him! Public confession and the fact that the early Fathers were indeed "fathers" in Christ, who were ordered by law to remain celibate in 306 A.D., were other deeply disturbing reflections.

Interrupting his deep contemplation, Gabriel reminded him that it was time to leave as they were about to witness the martyrdom of an Apostolic Father of the early Church.

ST. POLYCARP
(Disciple of John)

"And so I can describe the very place in which the blessed Polycarp used to sit as he discoursed, and his goings out and his comings in, and his manner of life, and his personal appearance, and the discources which he made to the people, and how he would describe his intercourse with John and the rest who had seen the Lord, and how he would relate their words."

(Irenaeus, *Letter to Florinus*)

Chapter 6

156 A.D.

All at once, Carter found himself at the scene of a cruel persecution. The massive crowd had just witnessed the torture of many Christians being thrown to the lions, and they now clamored for the death of the **Bishop Polycarp,** who had previously fled but was brought back by a very reluctant proconsul who was most anxious to save him. Polycarp was a disciple and companion of John, the Apostle of Jesus. He was the Bishop of Smyrna and later collected the letters of Ignatius, which have become a part of Church history and Tradition. *The Martyrdom of St. Polycarp* has furnished history with a vivid account of the death of this Apostolic Father. Gabriel then spoke of a letter written by St. Irenaeus to Florinus. "In this letter, Irenaeus describes the personal appearance of Polycarp, and the things that Polycarp related to him that were lessons of his childhood. As Polycarp spoke, his words were not put down on paper, but Irenaeus placed them in heart. Yet, Irenaeus recorded that by the grace of God, he could recall them exactly to mind. The following indicates the importance of this apostolic Father in the early Catholic Church."

> "In the preservation and continuation of such traditions and institutions, Polycarp must have had a considerable part; thus, for later generations, he has become an important link between the apostolic age and the early Catholic Church with respect to apostolic tradition and succession." (*Encyclopedia Britannica*)

As the persecution was about to begin, the proconsul continued to urge the aged Polycarp to deny Christ, but he would not recant. The crowd insisted that he be burned alive. Since the flames did not immediately engulf him, to end his sufferings, the executioners thrust a sword into his body. Positioning the disciple of John in the middle of the blaze, a centurion then burned his body, which was a custom of the Gentiles.

Gabriel said to Carter: "Here we have one of the most important martyrs in the history of the Church and yet you never mention his name to your people. Polycarp was a disciple of John. Furthermore, history records that his bones were more valuable than precious stones, and this is why **relics** are sacred to Catholics. He is an Apostolic Father and a crucial figure in the line of Apostolic Succession. Sacred Tradition supports the Bible that you now hold in your hand, for it indeed records the importance of 'relics.'"

The archangel swiftly found several clear scriptural passages in *Matthew* 14:36, *Mark* 5:30; *Acts* 19:11-12; and *2 Kings* 13:21 to show the importance of holy relics. The irrefutable fact is that history also records this early veneration. Even encyclopedias acknowledge as much.

"Before we depart this scene, I wish to make clear to you one other misconception you have of the Church, and that is that Catholics worship statues. God warned the idolatrous cults and forbid the 'worship' of pagan gods and images. However, two cherubs were on each end of the Ark of the Covenant (*Exodus* 25:18). The Lord was most pleased and consecrated Solomon's temple (*1 Kings* 9:3), which included sculptures of angels, lions and oxen, including two golden angels made of olivewood ten cubits high (*1 Kings* 6:23-28). Just as you do not worship the Statue of Liberty or the Lincoln memorial, neither do Catholics 'worship' statues of saints as they are only symbols and expressions of their faith in the intercession of the saints in Heaven, which is found in *Revelations* 8:3-4. And what of the 'bronze image of the serpent' that cured the afflicted of Moses' time?" (*Num.* 21:6-9)

Reminding Carter that Protestants also use statues depicting the nativity scene during the Christmas season in their homes and in their churches, Gabriel said, "Catholics merely use them all year round due to their deep devotion and reverence for the 'communion of saints' in Heaven. However, the statues themselves are not worshipped in any way."

Knowing they were about to depart, Carter quickly turned to gather one last look at the spot where the martyred body of St. Polycarp had burned.

Chapter 7
160 A.D.

Engulfed in a sudden, brilliant light, Carter realized that he was now looking across a road to a particular spot on a hill where Christians were kneeling and praying. It was a gravesite or a *trophy* as it was sometimes called, and situated on a hill that would one day be known as Vatican Hill. Gabriel defined the reason for the veneration at this particular gravesite: "The altar of the future great basilica will be erected over this grave of Peter, thus making the words of Our Lord in *Matthew* 16:18-19: *Upon this rock, I will build My Church...* even more profound. Jesus called Peter the Aramaic name *Cephas* or *Kephas* which means 'rock' and again uses this name in *John* 1:42. The apostles also called Peter this new name in *Galatians* 2:9 and *1 Corinthians* 1:12, 3:22; 9:5, 15:5. The *Encyclopedia Britannica* reports:"

> "That in building it, he [Constantine I] believed himself to be honouring the actual grave of the apostle is *proved* by the formidable difficulties both moral and physical, which he was prepared to face in order to build it where he did, terraced out from steep hillside and obliterating a large and predominantly pagan cemetery that was still in active use...On the other hand, it has been proved that since about the year 160, this spot has been the object of continuous veneration, a veneration which early hardened into a firm conviction that this was in fact the burial spot of the apostle. It

has moreover been shown that the surviving features of the 2nd-century shrine are consistent with, and in several respects most readily explained by, the hypothesis that it marks the site of an actual burial, which was disturbed by the builders of the adjoining mausoleum and which the contemporary Christian community rightly or wrongly identified as that of Peter. Whether, a century after Peter's death, they had good grounds for their belief cannot be decided; but that the shrine they erected became the centerpiece of Constantine's basilica and that, situated directly beneath the high altar of the present church, it has remained the subject of continuous veneration for more than 18 centuries is a demonstrable historical *fact*." (*Encyclopedia Britannica*)

Carter asserted, "but I have always been taught that Peter was never in Rome." "No," replied Gabriel, "that is incorrect. Look..." The *Encyclopedia Britannica* states:

"Though his having been in Rome is in Peter's case even less explicitly attested than in Paul's, the evidence is nevertheless such as cannot seriously be called into question. That the Prince of the Apostles was in fact in Rome seems to be established beyond all reasonable doubt." (*Encyclopedia Britannica*)

Gabriel illuminated further: "Carter, as you read the New Testament, you will see that Peter's leadership is acknowledged throughout the Bible in many ways. He is usually listed first among the disciples and is usually the spokesman for them. Sometimes he is simply referred to as 'Peter and those who were with him' as in *Luke* 9:32. The temple tax was paid for only by Jesus and Peter with a shekel miracuously found in the mouth of a fish (*Matthew* 17:27). Moreover, as Jesus prepared to ascend into Heaven, just as God always provided a visible shepherd for His people in the Old Testament, Jesus handed over His flock to Peter, (*John* 21:15-17). Previously, Peter had denied Jesus three times. In the end, he affirmed Him three times. Therefore, the Jerusalem Bible makes this note on this passage from John which established the Papacy:

> *John* **21:15-17:** "It is possible that the triple repetition indicates a contract made in due form according to semitic custom, c.f. *Genesis* 23:3-16." (*The Jerusalem Bible*)

"The simplicity of God's plan should seem more evident to you now, more than ever," Gabriel continued in a quiet, almost dejected voice. "Why have you never regarded the role of the Pope as the visible shepherd on earth to maintain unity for His Church after the Lord handed over His flock to Peter and then ascended into Heaven? In the Old Testament, God always provided strong visible shepherds like Moses, Abraham and David to lead His people. Why can you not receive the Kingdom of God like a child to understand that after the Lord ascended, surely He would not leave His sheep to argue amongst themselves over His words, as to what He truly meant? His flock would have scattered immediately! Please read what is written in scripture in *John* 10:1-16, keeping in mind that Jesus handed over the keys to the kingdom of Heaven to Peter."

Appearing quite pleased that Carter was listening so attentively and trying to logically reason all that he was presenting to him, Gabriel said, "Yes, the Lord appointed a visible leader, a 'fisher of men.' It was the disciples who went fishing 'with' Peter, and it was Peter who dragged the full net of 153 fish ashore without the net breaking in the very last chapter of *John* 21:1-25! The *New American Bible* footnote reports that Jerome asserted that Greek zoologists catalogued 153 species of fish, and it refers also to *Ezekiel* 47:10. Notice that 'fish and bread' were already mysteriously on the shore 'before' the fishing net was even drawn in. Jesus was then revealed to the disciples a third time! The Lord then established His verbal contract with Peter, turning over His flock to Him before He ascended. You will understand all when you compare *John* 21:19 to *John* 13:36."

It was as if a distant and obscure picture were suddenly becoming well-defined and Carter quietly acknowledged: "Perhaps my prejudice against the Catholics was so vast that my heart had hardened to the point of complete intolerance. Maybe I was blinded from the truth because of the fact that I never bothered to search for the reasons for their beliefs. I merely relied on information supplied by anti-Catholic writers. The problem now seems to be more evident. It was not the information I was given that is of any significance, but the verses and historical facts that were completely unknown to me that are relevant!"

Radiant and nodding his approval of the self-analysis Carter was making, Gabriel smiled. Once again, the pair resumed their heavenly journey to another time and place.

"Irenaeus, the most important theologian of the second century developed the Mary-Eve antithesis in the context of this theology of recapitulation... As the human race fell into bondage of death by means of a virgin, so it was rescued by a virgin."

(*Encyclopedia of Early Christianity*)

Chapter 8

180 A.D.

Instantly, they were in Gaul, in the city of Lyons. Sitting at a long writing table was one of the most learned, most discerning and most distinguished among the early heads of the Church. An Apostolic Father of the early Church, **Irenaeus** was a disciple of St. Polycarp, and the Bishop of Lyons (177-202). He was martyred in the year 202. In his account, *Against Heresies,* Irenaeus saw the church of Rome as the outstanding Apostolic See, "one with which all must be in agreement." Irenaeus also stressed the importance of the Tradition handed down through a Church, which although disseminated throughout the world, "believes these things just as if she had but one soul and one and the same heart; and harmoniously she proclaims them and teaches them and hands them down, as if she possessed but one mouth."

After speaking briefly with Gabriel, Irenaeus stood erect and carefully reiterated the utmost importance of referring to "Sacred Tradition" to uphold the truth of the *Word* when there were disputes, thus keeping the unity of the Church in tact. Speaking directly to Carter, Irenaeus said...

> "If there should be a dispute over some kind of question, ought we not have recourse to the most ancient Churches in which the Apostles were familiar, and draw from them what is clear and certain in regard to that question? What if the Apostles had not in fact left writings to us? Would it not be necessary to follow the order of tradition, which

was handed down to those to whom they entrusted the Churches?" (Irenaeus, *Against Hersies*)

As Irenaeus returned to his writing, Gabriel and Carter walked to the other side of the room. From there, they carefully observed this most influential Father of the Church who relentlessly stood up to heresy in the early Church with great fervor. Gabriel divulged the significance of Irenaeus' explanation in the role of Mary in the Church, a role sadly misunderstood, even by Catholics. He also revealed that like Justin Martyr (100-165 A.D.), Irenaeus also referred to Mary as the "New Eve" when he faced the heretical Gnostics in two of his Mariological doctrines about the Eve-Mary antithesis, *Against Heresies* and *Proof of the Apostolic Preaching*.

Confirming this important belief, Gabriel said, "I was the archangel sent to Mary, who was filled with grace and blessed among all women. She said 'yes' in complete obedience to the Father; *May it be it done to me according to your word'* (*Luke* 1:38). The parallel between *Genesis* 3:15 and the Annunciation in *Luke* 2 makes it clear that both Eve and Mary were virgins and both had a part in God's plan of salvation history."

> "Irenaeus, the most important theologian of the second century developed the Mary-Eve antithesis in the context of this theology of recapitulation...
> In this plan of salvation, Mary's role parallels that of Eve. Eve, while yet a virgin *disobeyed* and became the cause of death for herself and the whole human race. Mary, as a virgin, *obeyed* and became a cause of salvation for herself and the whole human race...As the human race fell into the bondage of death by means of a virgin, so it was rescued by a virgin (*Adversus Haeresos* Vol. 5: 19, 1)." (*Encyclopedia of Early Christianity*)

"Carter," the angel stated, "Mary was, through her obedience to God, the **cause** of salvation for herself and the whole human race. Both virgins had free will, the will to obey or disobey God. However, because Paul calls Jesus the 'New Adam' in *Romans* 5, we cannot have a New Adam without a 'New Eve.' This is why many of the early fathers and doctors of the Church taught that Mary was immaculately conceived, preserved for God's plan of salvation. St. Ambrose [340-397] will later earnestly profess, 'Adopt me, however, not from Sarah, but from Mary, so that it might be an incorrupt virgin, virgin by grace free from all stain of sin.' "

Gabriel once again expounded on the importance of the unique role of Mary to Carter. "Remember, it is scriptural and prophetic that Mary said, *My soul magnifies the Lord* during her visit with her cousin Elizabeth at the Song of the Magnificat. Perhaps if you could picture Mary as a large magnifying glass, then when you peer through her soul, you will see Jesus even greater than ever before through her intercession. Why do you ask your friends to pray *for* you and *with* you and yet, you refuse to ask Mary to do the same thing? Your friends are only taking the place of Mary when they pray for you."

Reflecting on all Gabriel said, the evangelist still appeared somewhat puzzled and inquired, "I have heard Mary referred to as the Ark of the 'New' Covenant. Why is this title used?"

The penetrating answer was profound: "Read scripture, including *Hebrew* 9:1-4; 1 *Samuel* 21:2-7, and *Exodus* 30:1-6. You will readily discover that the Ark of the Old Testament contained the word and the bread of God, (Ten Commandments and the pot of manna). It was lined in and out with pure gold and had angels on each side."

"In the New Testament, Mary became the Ark of the New Covenant because Jesus is also called the word (*John* 1) and the Living Bread (*John* 6:51). The lining of gold compares to her immaculate womb which beheld the fullness of God, and thus, she became a 'living tabernacle' for the nine months she carried Jesus. My presence before her at the Annuciation fulfills the comparison of the 'angels' of the first Ark. Furthermore, refer to 2 *Samuel* 6:2-19 in the Old Testament as David danced before the entrance of the Ark into

Tabernacle: Ark of the Old Covenant
(Hebrews 9:1-5; 1 Samuel 21:2-7)

Ark (rear)   Altar of Incense (center)   Table of Shewbread (right)

Mary: Ark of the New Covenant

And the angel being come in said unto her, "Hail, full of grace, the Lord is with thee: blessed art thou among women." (Luke 2:26-28)

Douay-Rheims Bible
"Vulgate"—English Translation

Jerusalem. This correlates to the leap of John the Baptist in Elizabeth's womb during the visit of Mary and Elizabeth in *Luke* 2. This compelling similarity also confirms the presence of 'life' in the womb because one child acknowledged the presence of the other Child, Jesus the Lord, while each were still in the wombs of their mothers! This beautiful scriptural passage supports the Church's position against abortion."

Gabriel's comparison became even more compelling: "In the Old Testament, Jeremiah hid the ark (*2 Macabees* 2:4-8) and declared that the place would be unknown until God gathered His people together. In the New Testament, *Revelations* 2:17 reveals, *To him who conquers, I will give some of the 'hidden' manna...* Remember that the Ark contained the pot of manna, the heavenly bread of God! Then *Rev.* 11:19 describes the ark that could once again be seen in Heaven among lightning, voices and an earthquake. Read on, but please realize that there were no verse numbers as John wrote this book; therefore, the very next verse, *Revelation* 12:1-18 describes a great sign appearing in Heaven—a *Woman clothed with the sun,* who gave birth to a son who was taken up to God and His throne. Some interpret this 'woman' to be the Church, but this would suggest that the Church gave birth to the Son when the opposite is true! The Son established His Church and thus, the 'woman' is Mary as Pope John Paul II affirms in his encyclical *Mother of the Redeemer* (3/25/87). Therefore, the manna is 'hidden' in the Old Testament Ark and also hidden in Mary, the New Testament Ark because it takes great 'faith' to believe the words of the Living 'manna' of *John* 6:51-59."

Since scripture revealed that Mary had announced in her song of the Magnificat that *all generations would call her blessed* (*Luke* 1:48), Carter felt agitated that he had completely ignored her. He longed to discuss her role in Scripture with her, and maybe even ask for her unconditional forgiveness for not loving her as he should have. Realizing these thoughts, Gabriel said, "The Blessed Virgin Mary is

'Queen of Heaven' in the family of God, and you are her child. Just as your mother forgives you, she too loves all of her children, no matter what their faith or whether the love is returned to her. All she asks of God's children is one simple, yet quite profound request, *Do whatever He tells you.* (*John* 2:5).

Chapter 9

200 A.D.

Again, the sudden flash of light and all at once, they were present at a baptismal ceremony, and Carter was astonished to see infants being baptized along with adults. The archangel assured Carter: "In the early Church, being **born again** had nothing to do with a spiritual conversion. Jesus was speaking of Baptism with water in *John* 3:3-5 and nothing more, Carter! Even as far back as the first century, encyclopedias confirm this simple fact. Christians did not repeatedly ask other Christians if they were 'born again' or 'saved' because being born again was simply Baptism. Observe the following..."

> "On the basis of these and similar declarations by the writers of the New Testament, it may be concluded that in the Christian community of the 1st century, baptism occupied a place of great importance and was regarded essential to the new birth and to membership in the Kingdom of God. The Gospel of John claims the authority of Jesus Christ Himself for this interpretation of baptism: *Unless one is born of water and the Spirit, he cannot enter the kingdom of God.*" (*Encyclopedia Britannica*)

> "The strong emphasis on the necessity of baptism was reinforced by *John* 3:3-5, which was the favorite baptismal text of the early church. Only in some Gnostic circles was there a depreciation

of the importance of baptism..." (*Encyclopedia of Early Christianity*)

Reminding him of the words of Justin, Gabriel said, "Justin stressed this point in his *First Apology* of 150 A.D. The term 'reborn' merely meant baptism with water and nothing else..."

> **(150 A.D.)** Justin Martyr: "Then they are led by us to a place where there is water; and there they are reborn in the same kind of rebirth in which we ourselves were reborn...For Christ said, 'Unless you be reborn, you shall not enter into the kingdom of Heaven'...The reason for doing this, we have learned from the Apostles." (*First Apology*, 150 A.D.)

Amazed, Carter looked once again at the "born again" passage from *John* 3:3-5 mentioned by the encyclopedia. His very soul seemed to cry out in complete disbelief, and yet an exhilaration settled in as his eyes disclosed God's truth. Words seemed to gently lunge toward him as Gabriel urged him to read further down to the end of the chapter and even further along into *John* 4. Gabriel said, "You can see that when Jesus ended His conversation with Nicodemus, Jesus and His disciples went into the land of Judea and baptized (*John* 3:22). The belief that 'born again' was a 'believer's baptism' and a spiritual conversion by a conscious decision of faith did not occur until the middle ages! Carter, let us once again refer to our references. If you check historical references, you will find that another group of reformers alongside the 'magisterial' leaders at Wittenburg, Zurich and Geneva introduced a radically new outlook into the doctrine and practice of baptism. These were the Anabaptists. The hostility of the Anabaptists to the union of church and state caused them to look for a pure church, into which one would come, not *automatically* by birth and infant baptism, but *consciously* by the decision of faith. This view of the church and of the individual represented a fundamental break with the baptismal tradition sketched above. Instead of infant baptism, the Anabaptist insisted upon believer's baptism, i.e., a baptism that followed faith and was not thought to create faith. You will find this is the wording found in the encyclopedia."

Implicating a certain sorrow in his voice because of Carter's belief in adult baptism only, Gabriel rationalized, "plainly, you can see that infants were also 'reborn' and belonged to the Kingdom in the early Church. Have you not read what Peter said in the Book of Acts?"

Acts **2:38-39:** *repent and be baptized everyone of you in the name of Jesus Christ...for the promise is to you and to your children and to all that are far off, everyone whom the Lord Our God calls to him...*

Persevering with this line of thought, Gabriel concluded with a Bible verse: "Our Lord Jesus Himself said, *Let the children come to me and do not prevent them; for the kingdom of heaven belongs to such as these.* Documents of the early church confirm that infants were indeed baptized...My friend, St. Cyprian of Carthage and his colleagues in council wrote a letter to Fidus in A.D. 251 concerning infant baptism."

"As to what pertains to the case of infants, you said that they ought not to be baptized within the second or third day after birth, and that the old law of circumcision must be taken into consideration, and that you did not think that one should be baptized and sanctified within the eight days after his birth. In our council, it seemed to us far otherwise. No one agreed to the course which you thought should be taken. Rather, we all judged that the mercy and grace of God ought to be denied to no man born." (*Letter of Cyprian and His Colleagues,* 215/252 A.D.)

"St. Augustine likewise made use of baptism in his controversy with the Pelagians, arguing that baptism conferred supernatural grace upon those who received it, whether infants or adults, and that it thus expunged the stain of original sin from them." (*Encyclopedia Britannica*)

Though the evangelist had preached against children being baptized, the fact remained that even infants were often permitted this rite in the early Church. The majority of Christians mentioned in the Bible were adults at the time of their conversion. Even in the early Church, many received their baptism as adults. However, the practice of baptizing infants indeed existed in the early Church, although in the middle ages, the heretical Waldenses eventually denied it and many of the reformers followed suit.

Before they moved on, Gabriel disclosed that there was one person that he wanted Carter to hear first hand. They began leisurely strolling towards a large square in the center of the city. Directing Carter's attention to the individual addressing the crowd, Gabriel disclosed that he was none other than *St. Clement of Alexandria*, director of a school of catechumens, who was giving a strict teaching on "faith" from his historical *Stromateis* or *Miscellanies:*

"When we hear, 'Your faith has saved you,' we do not understand [the Lord] to say simply that they will be saved who have believed in whatever manner, even if *works* have not followed. To begin with, it was to the Jews alone that He spoke this phrase, who had lived in accord with the law and blamelessly, and who had lacked only faith in the Lord." (Clement of Alexandria, *Stromateis,* 202 A.D.)

Studying the evangelist's reaction to the additional knowledge entrusted to him, Gabriel firmly declared: "You see, the early Fathers not only baptized children as well as adults, but good works were indeed necessary. The adult applicants for Baptism were called catechumens and entered a period of instruction that lasted two or three years before they could be baptized and confirmed by the bishop on Holy Saturday. These candidates for confirmation were introduced only gradually into the revealed truths of the Catholic faith and were required to pledge not to disclose these truths to pagans. "At first, because of the great persecution of the early Christians, Mass was celebrated in the houses of wealthy converts, and also over the tombs of martyrs in the catacombs. Later, the custom developed of placing relics of the martyrs in the altars of church. However, when Christianity became legal by the Edict of Milan of 313 A.D., basilicas such as St. John Lateran (324 A.D.) were erected. The life of the Early Christian centered around the Eucharist, the Holy Mass. However, never did these first Christians believe that it was only 'faith' that saved you. Even St. Ignatius wrote to Polycarp as early as 110 A.D.:

> " 'Let your works be as your deposited withholdings, so that you may receive the back-pay which has accrued to you.' (Ignatius, 110 A.D.)

"Notice that the first Christians also trace a cross on their foreheads. The *Encyclopedia of Early Christianity* reports that this custom was early and was incorporated into the liturgy. In the second century, *'The Acts of Peter'* describes Theon's baptism as 'washed and signed with thy holy sign.' "

Before Carter even had a chance to respond, they were once again off to travel to another period in time. "You still have much to learn," the angel confided as they left the gathering in the square.

Chapter 10

383 A.D.

With a sudden flash the evangelist now found himself in a small room with **Jerome**, the *Doctor of Sacred Scripture,* who had just been commissioned by Pope Damasus to interpret the various Latin translations. The *Encyclopedia Britannica* states: "The outcome of this commissioning was the *Vulgate*, which was the Bible of the Western Church for more than a millennium."

However, the Bible was not the subject the angel wanted to discuss with Carter. He was well aware that there was still a Bible verse that was on the minister's mind. Though he had accepted the comparison of Mary to the Old Testament Ark of the Covenant, the fact remained that Carter was knowledgeable in specific Bible verses that he had memorized and repeated relentlessly. Therefore, there remained one last subject that would be difficult for him to completely accept.

As he stood near a window gazing out upon the quiet fields on the outskirts of Rome, Jerome appeared immersed in deep thought. It was at this point that Gabriel decided to permit Jerome to address Carter directly, and after privately speaking together, Carter observed Jerome nodding in agreement. This striking figure of a man walked directly toward him and said, "Gabriel has summarized his heavenly mission from God. Before you leave this period in history, the days of the early Church, you must comprehend a grave error the people of your century still carry forth. This is that the Mother of God had *other* children! Refer to history and you will discover that Athanasius, Bishop of Alexandria and a Father and Doctor of the Church defended the perpetual virginity of Mary when he referred to her as 'ever-virgin' in his *Discourse Against the Arians*. Fiercely, I have just answered Helvidius when he attacked the perpetual virginity of Mary in my writing, *Against Helvidius*, which will be recorded in Church history for all Christians. Therefore, if you also hold this position, you are aligning your beliefs with those of the Arians of the early Church because of flagrant interpretations of scripture."

Now speechless and absolutely motionless, Carter could not seem to recover his emotions to generate any comment whatsoever. In front of him stood the *Father of Biblical Science*, who had given the entire Christian world the *Vulgate*, the pivotal foundation for the many translations that would eventually begin to evolve eleven hundred years later. Even the language of the Protestant reformers is incomprehensible without the knowledge of the *Vulgate* according to current encyclopedias.

Grievously, the evangelist pondered, "The Bible that I now carry so reverently depended greatly upon Jerome, who is now positioning my beliefs with the heretics of the early Church."

Jerome quickly resumed his justification of this belief, and eagerly defined the fact that the first Christians had always believed in the perpetual virginity of Mary. Clarifying this line of reasoning with simple logic, he said: "Previously, there was actually no need to defend her! Only when heresy arrived within the midst of Our Lord's sheep did we as apologists rouse ourselves to steadfastly defend the Blessed Mother. Many basilicas were dedicated to her, and her images were discovered in the catacombs dating back to the 2nd and 3rd centuries. Furthermore, nowhere in the Bible will you find any other children listed for the mother of Jesus, which greatly differs from the description of the other women under the cross or at the tomb of Our Lord, who are listed as, *'the mother of...'* The words are only recorded as, *and the brothers of Jesus*. Do you know why therein lies such great significance to this simple truth?"

Gabriel glanced towards Carter and informed him that

when translators began interpreting Holy Scripture over a thousand years later, they translated the Greek word *adelphos*, which also meant *relative, cousin* or *near kinsman* to be incorrectly interpreted as meaning *brothers*. Carter was then given a more current explanation:

> "In Hebrew, *ah* ordinarily translated 'brother,' but in practice, it expresses kinship in a larger sense, and less precisely than in English, on account of the absence of Hebrew terms for the different levels and degrees of relationship. Not only the sons of the same father, but all of the male members of the same family complex were called brothers...The New Testament, written in Greek, was composed by Semites, and the Aramaic background breaks through in very many places, so that the Greek word *adelphos* is more or less used in the larger sense of the Hebrew *ah* given above."
> (*New World Dictionary-Concordance*)

Emphatically, Jerome pointedly stressed, "This error in translation of the word *adelphos* thus caused much of the confusion for Christians of the future Church." On the other hand, Jerome's fears were alleviated when Gabriel assured him that the English translation of his Latin *Vulgate*, (the *Douay-Rheims Bible* of our day), had remained fairly constant in adhering to Jerome's interpretation. This English version was apparently an earnest attempt to achieve a sense of complete authenticity as compared to other English translations, although the angel rationalized that as with all Bible translations, even future revisions of the *Douay-Rheims* would be anticipated and added: "Jerome, allow me to confirm that the 'Preface' of the Douay-Rheims Bible indicated that you had access to Hebrew and Greek scriptures that are no longer in existence. Therefore Carter, will you then trust Jerome's translation before others...?"

> "The *Douay-Rheims Bible* is a scrupulously faithful translation into English of the Latin *Vulgate*

which St. Jerome (342-420) translated into Latin from the original languages... Besides being a towering linguistic genius, he was also a great saint, and he had access to ancient Hebrew and Greek manuscripts of the 2nd and 3rd centuries, which have since perished and are no longer available to scholars today. St. Jerome's translation, moreover, was a carefully, word-for-word rendering of the original texts into Latin." (*Douay-Rheims Bible*, "Preface")

Gabriel then encouraged Carter, "Please refer to *Matthew* 13:55 in this Douay-Rheims version. You will observe that it uses the word 'brethren' and not 'brother.' Your King James Version also correctly uses the word 'brethren.'" Seemingly relieved, Jerome was smiling as Gabriel persevered, "The Douay-Rheims 'footnote' is faithful to Jerome's original Latin translation because it is written as follows:

"*Matthew* 13:55: His brethren. These were the children of Mary, the wife of Cleophas, sister to our Blessed Lady, and therefore, according to the usual style of the Scripture, were called brethren, that is, near relations to our Saviour." (*Douay-Rheims Bible*)

Resuming his explicit clarification of the phrase, "brothers of Jesus," St. Jerome illustrated in great depth that the key figure to this puzzle which only surfaced during the period of the Reformation, is the disciple, **James the Less.** Jerome persisted: "History will record me as avowing this disciple to be a *cousin* of Our Lord. Even the 2nd century historian Hegesippus contended this same belief. If you would only cross-reference *all* of the Bible verses of the three women during and after the crucifixion, you would determine that the second Mary, (the one described as the 'sister' of the mother of Jesus, *John* 19:25), was the wife of Cleophas (Alphaeus) and was also the mother of James the Less and other children whose names correspond to those listed as the 'brothers' of Jesus. Therefore, this disciple and his brothers were only *cousins* or relatives of the Lord. The *Encyclopedia Britannica* will also confirm that the words I have just spoken to you will live on..."

Providing intricate details from scripture that current day ministers overlooked because of prejudice, Gabriel defined this important belief of the early Church: "Jesus was laid in a tomb in which no one had ever been laid (*Luke* 23:53). On Palm Sunday, He entered Jerusalem riding on an ass that no one had ever ridden, and the road was spread with cloaks and palms (*Mark* 11). Thus, His Blessed Mother's womb was also 'reserved' for Him alone because it became His sacred throne. Many theologians compare the emergence of Christ from the sealed tomb (*Matthew* 27:66, 28:1-6), and His going through locked doors (*John* 20:19), to the penetration of light through glass. Even St. Jerome wrote of this, in a letter to Pammachius in 392 A.D. as well as St. Augustine in a letter to Volusian, dated 412 A.D. Therefore, the fact remains that Mary was a virgin at the birth of Jesus, but she also remained a virgin in giving birth to Christ, the Saviour. The fullness of God cannot have existed in anything less! My words to Mary were, *Hail...full of grace!* (*Luke* 1:18, *Douay-Rheims Bible*). To be 'full' means there is no room left for anything else...brimming to the top! My mission for you is to thoroughly understand this because Mary is indeed honored and loved as a beloved role model of the Church, the perfect disciple who said, 'Yes' to God. However, she has been maligned by many Christians, even Catholics, who wish to ignore her perpetual virginity. In his *Commentary of the Whole Bible*, Matthew Henry listed the author of the *Epistle of James* as 'the other James, the son of Alphaeus, who was cousin-german to Christ, and one of the twelve apostles.'"

Folding his hands gently under his chin and closing his eyes, Jerome sighed and gently massaged his forehead, restraining his utter despair over this belief which he considered so very offensive. He appeared as though he were in great anguish as he opened his eyes once again and resumed his

PERPETUAL VIRGINITY OF MARY
("The East Gate")
"And he brought me back to the outer gate of the sanctuary, which faces east; and it was shut. And he said to me, 'This gate shall remain shut; it shall not be opened, and no one shall enter by it; for the Lord, God of Israel has entered by it; therefore, it shall remain shut. Only the prince may sit in it to eat bread before the Lord; he shall enter by way of the vestibule of the gate, and shall go out by the same way."
(*Ezekiel* **44:2-3**)

defense of Mary's title of "ever-virgin"; "My young friend, if you will only examine God's Word in *Ezekiel* 44:2, you will readily see that the *East Gate* which the Lord is prophesied to enter is to forever remain closed, and none *shall pass through it, except the God of Israel alone.* Likewise, the womb of Mary beheld God and could hold no other...for the gate closed. St. Ambrose confronted the serious error of Bonosus on this issue with this same verse from the Old Testament. Please note with certainty that in this regard...it is a fact that the *east gate* of Jerusalem or so-called 'Golden Gate' is indeed closed, and it will remain closed even in the 20th century. The 'brothers' of Jesus were only His relatives. Inaccurate future translations of the Hebrew and Greek scriptures lend heavily to your belief that Jesus had brothers. I fully understand your consternation over this."

Carter still seemed puzzled and asked: "What about the verse in *Matthew* 1:23-25 which used the words *first-born* and *until?* Doesn't this imply that there were other children of Mary and therefore, the existence of brothers of Jesus?"

"Unfortunately," the angel responded, "some are refusing to accept the teachings of the early Fathers of the Church when they quote the words, *first-born son* to refute her perpetual virginity. Surely the knowledge of the early Fathers of the Church should far outweigh the reasoning of those living in your time because they lived only a short time after the death of Jesus. For ancient Jews, the term only meant, 'the child that opened the womb' as in *Exodus* 13:2 and *Numbers* 3:12. This child occupied a place of privilege and the term was used under Mosaic Law. It meant that the child was to be sanctified as in *Exodus* 34:20. The first male son was always determined to be the 'first-born' even if the child was the only son of the marriage. Author Karl Keating reports that there is a historical funeral inscription in Egypt which refers to a woman who died during childbirth, the infant being, 'first-born' son!

"As for the word *until,* this only meant that the action did not happen up to a certain point. It did not imply that the action then happened later! An example of this can be found in *Genesis* 8:7 which reveals that the raven that Noah released *went forth and did not return till the waters were dried up upon the earth.'* The raven never returned—only the dove returned! Carter, what will Jesus say to those who despise His mother so much when they meet Him at Heaven's gate? Profoundly, Mary has proclaimed to mankind the purpose of her mission to God's children: *Do whatever He tells you...''*

Jerome had been carefully listening, intent on his visitor's complete understanding of Mary's unique role in the Church. Feeling as though the young man did now indeed fully comprehend the difficult explanations, Jerome bid the pair a fond farewell.

With even greater clarity, Carter could now envision her role in God's perfect plan of salvation for His children. The realization of the plan unfolded with the comparison of the Old Testament Eve to Mary, the *New Eve.* Opening the Bible, he prayerfully discerned that from the passages of the first Book of *Genesis* (3:15) to the last Book, *Revelations* (11:19 to the end of Chapter 12), the triumph of the victory over Satan was now more clear.

"Yes," Gabriel announced, "The gate closed, and the dragon will indeed be defeated by the seed of the woman...Our Lord and Saviour, the hidden manna, Jesus...but without the obedient 'yes' of Mary as she answered me on my momentous mission from God, the plan would not have proceeded. She is not only the Heavenly Mother of all God's children, but the perfect disciple and an example for all Christians to follow."

Pleased that his mission seemed to be progressing so successfully due to the genuine concern and willingness of Carter to carefully heed every single word that Gabriel spoke, the archangel's words seemed to almost reverberate. "Carter, before we leave this period in Church History, you may find it interesting that in the *Vulgate* of 387-404 A.D., Jerome translated the *Lord's Prayer* quite differently from the translations that appeared later during the Reformation and even later English translations. *Matthew* 6:11: *Give us this day our daily bread* was translated as 'Supersubstantial' bread by Jerome and also in the *Douay-Rheims Bible* of your day. This is because the Greek word *epiousios* is a word not found anywhere in classical or sacred Greek. This word in *Matthew* was so 'special' that it had to be broken down into the component parts of *epi*, which in Greek means respect, space, time, and *ousia* which means substance. This is why there were differences in translations during the reformation period and thereafter, because critics cannot determine just what it means. The 'supersubstantial bread' was the Eucharist, the 'Living' bread that Our Lord commanded us to eat for our eternal salvation. *John* 6:27 warns us that we should not work for food that perishes but for the food that 'endures' for eternal life. **Cyprian of Carthage** also spoke of the Eucharist as 'heavenly bread' to be given 'daily,' as early as **251 A.D.** in his treatise, *The Lord's Prayer.* Let us look at definitions from your own era."

> **Epiousios:** "The word translated *daily* is not found in Greek writings independent of Christian literature, except for one occurrence in a single papyrus, and its meaning and derivation have never been satisfactorily explained." (*The Interpreter's Bible*)

> **(Lord's Supper):** "A radical eschatological interpretation would in paraphrase read somewhat like this...'Give us today the foretaste of the *heavenly* banquet [daily bread]; rather, the bread for the morrow;....'" (*Encyclopedia Britannica*)

> **Supersubstantial:** "more than substantial; transcending the domain of matter; used especially with reference to the phrase in the Lord's prayer, *Matthew* 6:11, where the word *daily* in the King James version reads *supersubstantialis* in the *Vulgate*." (*Webster's New Twentieth Century Dictionary*)

"Carter, can you not see why Jerome translated this Greek word to be the Eucharist and translated it as *Give us this day our supersubstantial bread* in the *Vulgate*? According to the definition in *Webster's Dictionary*, the word seems to exist because of Jerome's interpretation of this distinctive and most extraordinary Greek word! From the earliest days of the Church, the recitation of the Lord's Prayer always held a privileged place in the liturgy of the Mass. It follows the Eucharistic Prayer and precedes the 'sign of peace.' "

Silently, Carter prayed the Lord's Prayer, sifting it in his mind, and now it took on an entirely new meaning to him. Moving his lips as he prayed, he realized that it was a prayer about his salvation, not a prayer that pleads with God to provide his daily needs! "In fact," he responded, "I never realized that the words 'day' and 'daily' are redundant. 'Give us this day, our *supersubstantial* bread'...our *heavenly* bread!"

His face more radiant than ever, Gabriel exuded pure pleasure that the enlightment of God's Truth was now clear. "Yes, the Lord erases all doubt as to what this means. After He taught them the Lord's Prayer, He said, ...*do not be anxious about your life, what you shall eat or what you shall drink, nor about your body...* (*Matthew* 6;25). Likewise, the feeding of the 5,000 prefigured His explanation of the Eucharist in *John* 6, and yet this crowd who had already witnessed two miracles urged Him for more. He again forewarned them, *Do not labor for the food which perishes but for the food which endures to enteral life'* (*John* 6:27), and then explained the Eucharist, the third miracle that would ultimately 'test' their faith, but they walked away! Carter, have you walked away? We can help more of our brothers and sisters to not walk from the Lord if we can eliminate errors of interpretation that have separated us."

Chapter 11

400 A.D.

Addressing a large crowd was one of the greatest theologians of all times... **Augustine**, Bishop of Hippo, Father and Doctor of the Church. His extraordinary *City of God* incorporates a theology of history, and his remarkable sermons, letters and autobiographical information are priceless in the history of the early Church. His various writings had a strong and lasting influence on all Christian theology and philosophy:

> "If anyone says that faith merits the grace of doing good works we cannot deny it; rather we admit it most readily." (Augustine, *Letter to Paulinus of Nola*)

> "But in regard to those observances which we carefully attend and which the whole world keeps, and which derive not from Scripture but from Tradition, we are given to understand that they are recommended and ordained to be kept, either by the Apostles themselves or by plenary councils, the authority of which is quite vital in the Church." (*Letter of Augustine to Januarius,* 400 A.D.)

However, St. Augustine was now eloquently speaking to the people about a place where we are "saved by fire." Carter listened intently as the theologian loudly proclaimed: "And because it is said that he shall be saved, little more is thought of that fire! Yet plainly, though we be saved by fire, that fire

"and because it is said that he shall be saved, little is thought of that fire! Yet plainly, though we be saved by fire, that fire will be more severe than anything a man can suffer in this life."
St. Augustine, [392-418 A.D.]
"Explanation of the Psalms"

will be more severe than anything a man can suffer in this life." (*Explanations of the Psalms*, 392-418 A.D.)

Looking quite puzzled, Carter leaned towards Gabriel and quietly asked, "What place is he talking about? Where can a man can be saved, but only through fire?" With great patience, the angel assured him that this place was *Purgatory*, a belief that Carter had frequently openly denounced.

Gabriel simply justified this belief of the early Church by stating that the Jews had always believed in praying for the dead. "Moreover," he said, "please recall the notable fact that Luther quickly eliminated seven books of the Bible during the Reformation. One of the first to vanish from scripture was *2 Maccabees*. Why? Because Luther did not like Confession or the thought of Purgatory because he wanted **assurance** of his salvation. Luther advised his friend Melanchthon to 'be a sinner and sin boldly, but believe more boldly still...' Now, according to Luther, the state of one's soul no longer depended on such beliefs, although they had been believed from **day one** of the Church.

"Luther, independent of all of the teachings of the early Fathers and Doctors of the Church, decided it was now 'faith alone' that was needed. This is why he labeled the early Apostolic Fathers 'infernal blasphemers' if they taught about a place where we are saved through fire (purgatory) and the importance of confession. However, sometimes he was forced to appeal to their writings when he disagreed with a fellow reformer's interpretation of scripture. In doing so, Luther was appealing to Sacred Tradition, and his theory of the 'Bible alone' was no longer a convincing argument.

"Carter, the passage from *Maccabees* is clear and concise; however, it conflicted with Luther's new enlightenment. The verse from *2 Maccabees* 12:43-45 reads: *It is therefore a holy and wholesome thought to pray for the dead; that they may be loosed from sins.* Unfortunately, Luther wanted assurance of his salvation, so he eliminated this book of the Bible which was a part of the *Septuagint*, the scriptures of all early Christians. My dear friend, your salvation can never be assured! *Therefore, let any one who thinks that he stands, take heed lest he falls (1 Corinthians* 10:12), for Paul said that we are saved in *hope* in his letter to the *Romans* 8;24-25 and repeatedly reminded us that the children of God must work out their salvation with fear and trembling. Yes, you should possess great hope and confidence that you are saved, but your reward can indeed be lost! You always seem to quote what Paul says, but what did the Lord say? Refer to *Matthew* 10:42 when Jesus said, *And whoever gives to one of these little one's even a cup of cold water because he is a disciple, should not lose his reward.* Luther wanted 'assurance' of his salvation and therefore, he dispensed with the belief in the purgation of the soul in preparation for our entrance into Heaven."

The evangelist seemed quite unwilling to accept the angel's words so readily and asked, "Did the early Fathers truly teach this? What Scripture verses did they refer to to verify such a place?" Gabriel answered: "Although the word 'purgatory' is not found in the Bible, neither will you find the words 'sacrament' or 'Trinity.' However, these beliefs developed and always existed in the early days of the Church. Though not called Purgatory, St. Augustine and Origen defined the doctrine more clearly for the early Christians by referring to *1 Corinthians* 3:11-15. This passage unquestionably speaks of laying a foundation upon which a Christian is to build with works of gold, silver, precious stones, wood, hay or stubble. Each man's work will become manifest *for the day will disclose it, because it will be revealed with fire, and the fire will test what sort of work each one has done...If any man's work is burned up, he will suffer loss; though he himself will be saved...but only as through fire.* My friend, do you not see? You will be saved, but first there is a purgation! Read *Hebrews* 12:22-24 regarding the 'just' made perfect. Jesus also said, *truly I say to you, you will never get out till you have paid the last penny* in *Matthew* 5:25-26. From what place are you escaping? It is not Hell, for a soul can never leave the bottomless pit once they have entered. The place is not Heaven, for this is your eternal reward! Then where is this place that the Lord is talking about...a prison where you can as yet be saved but must pay the last penny? A few verses later (vs. 48), He warns: *You therefore, must be perfect, as your heavenly Father is perfect."*

Once again, they listened in as Augustine taught the Christians about a place where some of them would be purged from their sins...

> "But the man who perhaps has not cultivated the land and has allowed it to be overrun with brambles has in this life the curse of his land on all his works, and after this life, he will have either purgatorial fire or eternal punishment [*habetit vel ignem purgationis vel poenam aeternam*]" (Augustine, *Genesis Defended Against The Manicheans,* 389 A.D.)

Continuing, Gabriel assured Carter: "The practice has always been taught. Tertullian (160-240 A.D.) spoke of anniversary Masses for the dead. St. Basil wrote in 370 A.D. in his *Homilies on the Psalms,* about a place where those with sins or the effects of sins are detained, for a soul may not be worthy of Heaven or Hell. As early as **202 A.D.,** Clement of Alexandria spoke of a discerning fire. The *Encyclopedia of Early Christianity* states: "Intermittently, too, early Christianity intimated that a person's fate may not be settled at death (only to be confirmed and enforced at the last judgment) and pictured divine punishment as a purifying fire, (cf. *Isaiah* 66:15-16; *Malachi* 3:2-3; *1 Corinthians* 3:11-15), purgative rather than punitive in force. Clement of Alexandria mentions instructive as well as punitive correction and speaks of a discerning fire that penetrates the soul."

As they prepared to leave, Gabriel turned toward Carter and stated, "Paul Whitcomb, a former Protestant says it best in his little book, *The Catholic Church Has The Answer."* He maintains: "If there is no Purgatory, but only Heaven for the perfect and Hell for the imperfect, then the vast majority of us are hoping in vain for life eternal in Heaven."

Proclaiming the indisputable fact that Augustine fiercely

Paul, The Apostle (Purgatory)

Now if any one builds on the foundation with gold, silver, precious stones, wood, hay, straw—each man's work will become manifest; for the Day will disclose it, because it will be revealed with fire and the fire will test what sort of work each one has done...If any man's work is burned up, he will suffer loss; though he himself will be saved, but only as through fire. (*1 Corinthians* 3:12-15) battled heresy within the Church, Gabriel cited several of the characteristics of 88 heresies and the many heretics mentioned by Augustine, including the Antidicomarites, who contradicted the perpetual virginity of Mary and the Jovinianists who taught that a man was not able to sin after he had received the 'bath of rebirth' [baptism] and also instructed his followers that there was no profit in fasting.

By this time, Carter was barely questioning further for he had long before realized that some of his personal interpretations of Holy Scripture had led him into convictions of various beliefs that were not believed in the early Church. Accepting the belief in Purgatory seemed quite effortless, but before he could reason any further, they were already on their way...Their heavenly journey was coming to an end.

Martin Luther, Wittenburg
Oct. 31, 1517

Painting by Hugo Vogel, 19th century

Chapter 12

1517

Carter suddenly found himself in Wittenburg, Germany and instantly knew that he would be present as Martin Luther nailed his 97 theses to the door of the university church. From afar, they observed the Augustinian priest whose initial intention was only to reform the Church, not to renounce it. How ironic that it was Halloween, October 31, 1517, a day that would shake the Church for all eternity, but certainly not from its solid foundation.

Unfolding his beautiful feathered wings for the first time, Gabriel stood majestically and yet sorrowfully he proclaimed: "The vine that John speaks of in Chapter 15 was broken when the former Roman Catholic priest, Martin Luther, openly maintained that the Church founded by Jesus Christ had fallen into error! The gates of Hell can never, ever prevail! Yes the Church was in need of reform and the Council of Trent, which met in 1545, defined Catholic doctrine and corrected areas where the Church of Jesus needed modification. Since the beginning of the Church, this is how the Church is maintained, through councils like the very first Council of Jerusalem described in the Book of *Acts*. Luther's advice denotes his new thinking when he said, **'Be a sinner, and sin boldly, but 'believe' more boldly still...'**"

Folding his wings neatly inward once again, Gabriel appeared more peaceful and far less distressed and said, "If the Gates of Hell had indeed prevailed, and it was supposedly Luther who saved the Church, then why did not every Christian remain a Lutheran after the Reformation? Confusion was the result. Beliefs were shattered as the parts of the Rock splintered into hundreds and hundreds of different doctrines. Instead of reforming the Church, the Church was reformed...the unity of beliefs vanished!"

> JESUS: *Truly, truly I say to you, he who does not enter the sheepfold by the door but climbs in by another way, that man is a thief and a robber; but he who enters by the door is the shepherd of the sheep. To him the gatekeeper opens...I am the door of the sheep...He who is a hireling and not a shepherd, whose own the sheep is not, sees the wolf coming and leaves the sheep and flees; and the wolf snatches them and scatters them...And I have other sheep, that are not of this fold; I must bring them also, and they will heed by voice.* **So there shall be one flock, one shepherd.**' " (*John* 10:1-16, RSV Bible)

Gabriel expounded on the importance of unity: "Carter, we need to recognize that if Jesus is the door of His sheep, the only person given keys in the entire *New Testament* was Peter, and he is the gatekeeper. The flock of Jesus was turned over to him in *John* 21. As you have already learned, just as Moses, Abraham and David were visible shepherds of the Old Testament, Peter became the visible shepherd on earth in the New Testament. *Isaiah* 5 speaks of the vineyard, *Woe to you who join house to house, who connect field to field...* Paul also left us these words in *1 Corinthians* 12:12-28 to stress the importance of unity: *For as the body is one, and has many members, and all the members of that one body being many are one body, so also is Christ...If the foot shall say, Because I am not the hand, I am not of the body...* As humans, your bodies could not function if your lips attempted to speak seven different languages at one time, if your eyes struggled to examine 50 different directions at once, if your ears tried to listed to everyone at one time, if your fingers wanted to do different chores all at once...No, Our Lord only wanted one Church! In 248-258 A.D., Cyprian reminded the followers of Christ that His robe had no seams...and at His Crucifixion, *they cast lots for it (John 19-23-24).*"

> "He that rends and divides the Church of Christ cannot possess the clothing of Christ..." (Cyprian, *The Unity of the Catholic Church,* 248-258 A.D.)

The staunch uncompromising position of the Church that Jesus established two thousand years ago and promised would always stand was emphasized by Gabriel: "Though many attempts to destroy the Church have been made throughout its two thousand years of existence, the eternal rigidity of the Church stands as a tangible fact of history. Though other beliefs and denominations have come and gone since the sixteenth century, the mighty Rock, the Catholic Church continues...and it continues to remain strong even as she enters into the twenty-first century. The Britannica reports..."

> "The papacy is the only institution that has existed continuously from the early Roman empire. The history of the papacy begins at the point when Jesus left his apostles. St. Peter, by virtue of the words spokn to him by Christ *(Tu es Petrus...'You are Peter,' etc. Matthew 16:18-19; cf. John 21:15)* and as a natural consequence of the role that he had already begun to play among his colleagues, can be seen to occupy a pre-eminent place from the beginning." *(Encyclopedia Britannica)*

Resuming his exhortation of the event that would change the history of the Church, Gabriel added, "even Luther was quite distraught over the results of the Reformation and exclaimed in his writings..."

> LUTHER: "This one will not hear of Baptism, that one denies the Sacrament, another puts a

world between this and the last day: some teach that Christ is not God, some say this, some say that: that there are about as many sects and creeds as there are heads. No yokel is so rude but when he dreams and fancies, he thinks himself inspired by the Holy Ghost and must be a prophet." (*Luther, De Wett III, 61*)

With his keen, penetrating perception, the angel instantaneously detected his traveling companion's thoughts as they raced through his head: "Carter, you are now wondering why the Reformation occurred at this point in history. At first, Luther's only desire was to be a very devout and holy Catholic priest, but he carried a seed of despair because unfortunately, his confessions sometimes lasted up to six hours and still he felt unworthy. Therefore, he began to search for different answers in Holy Scripture, in order that he would not experience such remorse for his sins.

"Through his own 'personal' interpretations of *Romans* 3:28 and other verses, Luther came to the ultimate conclusion that what Paul really meant was...that it was *Faith Alone* and not good works that saved a Christian! This was never believed by the first Christians or any Christian until the Reformation because Paul was only alluding to 'works of the law,' not works of charity! Regardless, he added the word *alone* to his own translation of the Bible. To further support his new doctrine, Luther labeled the Book of *James* as an 'epistle of straw' and attempted to eliminate it because it very explicitly conflicted with his new doctrine. As I have already revealed to you, he also attempted to remove other books from the Bible, such as *Maccabees*.

"During the Reformation period, every Christian could now read the Bible for themselves. Before this time, Bibles were scarce, since they had been beautifully handwritten, primarily by monks. It was considered a most holy act to chain these handwritten Bibles to reserve them 'for' the people, just as your generation chains telephone books to prevent theft or loss. However, after the printing press was invented and Christians were able to read the Bible for themselves, one of the reasons for the turmoil that ensued was they now believed Luther's teachings and interpretations of the Bible. He also taught them that 'anyone' could interpret Holy Scriptures, even a child. Thus, the peasants felt completely betrayed by the Church."

A poignant realization seemed to pierce Carter's very soul as he realized that although the Church was not perfect, Christ knew that the "Gates of Hell" would try to prevail and thus, He promised the apostles that the Paraclete, the Holy Spirit, would be with His Church always (*John* 14:15-17).

Reading his thoughts, Gabriel declared: "After establishing the papacy on Peter, the Rock, how could the Lord have then allowed His Church to become contaminated only a few hundred years later through false teachings? Would He have then patiently tolerated His visible shepherds, the popes, to disburse flagrant errors throughout the world until the time of the Reformation? It was impossible for Christ to break His promise! Jesus would not have allowed heretical beliefs to continue another twelve hundred years until the reformers saved His Church. History does not record the existence of any other church, any leader, or beliefs such as yours, that have continuously existed before or after the year 313 A.D., the period when Protestants believe the Church became corrupt with pagan influence! If you continue to believe this to be so, then what other church existed continuing the unbroken line of apostolic succession? When the Reformation did indeed occur, even the reformers could not agree! Before and after the year 313, the world had been 'Catholic' in all of the basic beliefs that I have revealed to you, and it has remained that way for 2,000 years. If leaders of a pure church existed after 313, and they supposedly had the same beliefs as yours, what were their names? Were they secluded in a cave from the year 313 A.D. until the Reformation transpired?"

Knowing that it was crucial that the evangelist fully comprehend the gravity of these beliefs, Gabriel strengthened this discussion: "No, the Church Our Lord established was so powerful, so visible, not even the Gates of Hell could prevail! It was not weak, nor so vulnerable and invisible that world history knows nothing of its existence! Even when Christians worshipped in the catacombs and were greatly persecuted, history indeed records their names and the beliefs for which they proudly died! It is imperative that you realize that regardless of this senseless argument, the current beliefs of some Protestants who teach this theory are not even similar to the beliefs of the so-called early, pure Church! There has never been any other Church..."

> "The authoritative theological meaning of the term 'Catholic' was most natural and came into general use at an early date. As heresies arose, it was used to distinguish the *true* church. Thus another definition of 'Catholic' arose, as meaning opposed to, limited, sectarian, heretical, or schismatic views or groups. This usage prevailed for almost 10 centuries, up to the final separation between East and West, after which the Eastern Churches distinguished themselves by using the title 'Orthodox.' This left the title 'Catholic' to be maintained (and claimed) by Rome and the West...The Roman Catholic Church has steadfastly maintained the ancient title, often without contest by other churches." (*Encyclopedia Americana*)

Carter silently reflected over the archangel's words. Many Protestants indeed believed that the Church became contaminated and "impure" under the reign of the emperor Constantine in 313 A.D., who issued the Edict of Milan which ordered the persecutions to desist and made it legal for Christians to openly worship God. Carter had repeatedly preached this from his pulpit.

Interrupting his thoughts, Gabriel said, "It is true that traces of pagan influence exist in every culture and religion. For example, the Christian customs of wearing wedding rings and displaying Christmas trees resulted from the influence of religions who worshipped other gods. The Christmas tree replaced the sacred oak of the god Odin in Norse mythology. Encyclopedias seem to believe that."

> "Evergreens, as symbols of survival, have a long association with Christmas festivities, probably dating from the eighth century when St. Boniface completed the Christianization of Germany and dedicated the fir tree to the Christ child to replace the sacred oak of Odin." *(Encyclopedia Britannica)*

It was of critical importance that Carter understand the Church's tenacious desire to erase Paganism: "Just as the Church has erected huge cathedrals directly over the earlier sites of pagan worship in Mexico and other countries, the Church also placed important feast dates on the same day as the pagans in the hope that this would 'replace' and eventually eradicate these days from their calendar, thus forcing them to accept Christianity more readily. Again, you must understand that if it were proven that the True Church became so contaminated with paganism that it was no longer the 'holy' Church of Jesus, then ultimately, this possibility would have meant that Christ had broken His promise! The Gates of Hell would have then prevailed and ruled His Church for another 1200 years until the Reformation 'saved' it! Is this possible?"

Elaborating, Gabriel continued in his lengthy summary against this faulty proposal of Protestants who believe the Church was pure only during the first 300 years of Church history. Gabriel again stressed that according to many historical documents and encyclopedias, "scripture and tradition were recognized as *parallel* norms..." and that *good works* were always necessary for our salvation. Furthermore, it was not *faith alone* that saved a Christian in the early Church. The Mass of 150 A.D. proved the *Real Presence* of Christ in the Eucharist and Baptism meant *born again,* with infants, children and adults being baptized. The books that Protestants call the *Apocrypha* were a part of the *Septuagint,* the scriptures of the early Christians, including Paul. The belief in *Purgatory* and also *confession* have always been a part of Church history and *celibacy* of the clergy was encouraged, practiced and then enforced in 306 A.D. at the council of Elvira. *Apostolic Succession* was vital to preserve the unity of the Church; therefore, Peter was indeed the first Bishop of Rome, the first Pope who, according to archaeologists is entombed under the altar of St. Peter's Basilica, making the words of Jesus *Upon this Rock...* most profound and fulfilling His very significant promise of *Matthew* 16:18-19. Mary, the woman of *Genesis* 3:15 and *Revelations* 12 was called the "New Eve" and lastly, holy *relics* were extremely important to the early Christians.

This was the pivotal point of his mission, for Gabriel genuinely wanted the facts that he had presented to solidify into logical reasoning: "Carter, in view of the knowledge that I have entrusted to you, you must fully comprehend that the belief that the Catholic Church became tainted **after** the year 313 A.D. would mean that while under the jurisdiction of the Papacy, this so-called corrupt Catholic Church presented to the whole world the canon of the Bible, the Holy Book that you now hold in your hand! Do you not see the simplicity of the whole matter? History confirms that it was the Roman Catholic Church that called councils and officially decided which Books were inspired. Did the Lord allow His Church to exist for another twelve hundred years in grievous error, teaching and establishing churches using the same sacred book that they themselves had assembled under the guidance of the Holy Spirit? Did the gates of Hell ever prevail? Additionally, please note that the official wording of the *Apostles Creed* that you often recite was formally presented by the Catholic Church after the date of 313 A.D. This creed continues to be recited by other Protestants in the twentieth century!"

Indicating the importance of not eliminating a belief just because a "word" was not found in the Bible, Gabriel simply pointed out that this does not mean that the early Christians did not believe in the doctrine or the concept of the belief.

The actual words *Trinity* and *sacrament* are *not* found in the Bible, and yet Protestants believe in these doctrines despite their dependence on the Bible alone theory. These words are the result of doctrines that developed gradually to describe beliefs that have always existed in the early Church because of scriptural interpretation. Carter seemed quite perplexed, but Gabriel relentlessly persevered along this line of thinking.

"Although all Christians believe in the doctrine of the 'Trinity,' this word cannot be found anywhere in the Bible. The dogma for the belief was formally defined in the 4th century at a Catholic council under the leadership of the Pope during a period in which you have taught that the Church was impure. The fact remains that a complete reliance on Sacred Tradition and Holy Scripture enabled these councils to officially set the criteria of the all important 'unity' of Christian orthodoxy."

Carter, with an open mind toward anything that might strengthen his life-long commitment to God, pondered the Angel's words. He certainly did not wish to abandon all of his beliefs without considerable discernment. Gabriel acknowledged his concerns.

Gabriel asked Carter to again consider his explanation of specific words that are used by many Christians, but are not found anywhere in the Bible, and then pointed out that despite a reliance on the Bible alone, the additional words *rapture, revival,* and *altar calls* are not found in Holy Scripture either. Thus the use of these words eliminates the "Bible alone" in reality and in theory. The difference between these words and those previously mentioned is that the latter were **never** used in the early Church, nor in Sacred Tradition and were never approved through any dogma or authority of the Church councils. Gabriel then justified the complete reliance on the Church and the Early Fathers for Bible interpretation as he announced: "An example of the importance of looking to the Church for Scripture interpretation to support what was always believed or what should be believed (due to the promise of Christ and the constant eternal presence of the Paraclete), would be the belief in 'the rapture,' a teaching that was totally unheard of before the nineteenth century. This teaching is the result of a theory of 'Dispensationalism' formed by John Nelson Darby, whose writings greatly impressed C. I. Scofield, author of the *Scofield Reference Bible*. 'The Rapture' to some Christians, particularly fundamentalists, highlights an event that purifies the world and allows them to ascend into Heaven without experiencing death or the Great Tribulation. Traditional Christian teaching has always affirmed through Holy Scripture that the Great Tribulation will occur first and even the 'elect' will suffer on earth during the Tribulation and that *for the elect's sake, those days shall be shortened* according to *Matthew* 24:22. It is then that the 'Second Coming' of Christ gloriously takes place in verses 27-31. This 'Second Coming of Christ' is what St. Paul alluded to in *1 Thessalonians* 4:15-17, a verse quoted by some Christians, along with *1 Corinthians* 15:51 to support their belief.

"To some Christians, this heavenly occurrence would seemingly transpire 'before' the Second Coming of Christ, instead of meaning His actual Second Coming. Called 'The Rapture,' this is a recent and drastic interpretation of scripture that was never believed before in the history of the Church. My point is that some Christians teach that if a word is not found in the Bible, the belief does not exist. However, the word 'rapture' is not found in the Holy Bible and yet some Bible Christians teach this doctrine through misinterpretation of scripture, and thus, dependence on the Bible alone theory rapidly disintegrates."

As their journey concluded, Gabriel yearned to expose a few more claims against the Church which made it appear as though it were the anti-church: "My friend, the period of the ecclesiastical Inquisitions is not to be confused with the Spanish Inquisitions; yet, it was certainly a very dark period in the history of Christianity. At first, the Inquisition was instituted to avert the many heretical beliefs that began to permeate the Church. The initial intentions were honorable because although the Albigensian wars had ended, the Albigensian heresies persisted. However, the persecution of heretics did not change during the Protestant Reformation, as even Luther, Melanchthon, and Calvin approved of using capital punishment for those they considered heretics. In fact, Calvin even wrote, 'Heretics are to be coerced by the sword' after he burned Michael Servetus at the stake. The Gates of Hell were undeniably attempting to prevail, but the promise of Jesus was not to be broken, for with the Council of Trent, the Church instituted stricter laws and corrected error."

Many denominations have also leveled the charge that the Catholic Church placed the Holy Bible on the "Index of Forbidden Books" at the Council of Valencia in 1229. Resuming the explanation, Gabriel said: "This is absolutely false and is a perfect example of how words and facts can be distorted that make the Catholic Church appear outrageously evil. In reality, the Index was not even established until 1543, three centuries later than the date given. There was no council in Valencia in the year 1229; however, there was a council held in Toulouse that addressed the issue of the Bible because the heretical Albigensians believed that Christ was only a man (among other heretical beliefs), and they were using unauthorized versions of the Bible to spread their radical views.

"The bishops at Toulouse indeed confronted this issue, but it was an isolated local action that confined the use of the Bible only in southern France until the Albigensian heresy ceased to exist. Various anti-Catholic authors never bother to verify their information with the Church! This grave error is just one example of how erroneous and terribly hurtful so-called 'facts' can spread and contributes to the false impression that the Church despises the Bible. It is a fact that when various inaccurate translations appeared during the Reformation, the Church was against these translations and sought to eliminate them because the Catholic Church is the 'mother' of the Bible and desires only to preserve the pure Word of God through interpretation according to the early Fathers.

"Throughout the ages, the Church has fought numerous barbarians to protect the Holy Bible and were it not for the Catholic Church, there would be no Bible in existence! At any Mass, you will observe that during the procession up the aisle to the altar, the Word of God is carried high in the air, kissed by the priest and revered more in the Catholic Church than at any other Christian service in existence."

The last words to Carter from the archangel were: "My new friend, I cannot impress upon you enough the consequences of believing what you read from anti-Catholic sources. You must always search for the truth yourself, and the truth is easily found. What have you learned from all I have shown you? Has my mission from God been triumphant? Can you now understand that some of your beliefs are not the same as the early Christians?"

For a moment, Carter was at a complete loss for words. His emotions ranged from skepticism, to remorse, to pure gratitude. Finally, he said with deep feeling: "My dear, dear angel. No words can ever express the indebtedness that I owe you for this heavenly journey. You have shown me human errors, and that I have listened to individual interpretations, rather than God's Word and the Tradition of all of the early Fathers I have encountered on my journey. The reality of the papacy, the visible shepherd appointed by Christ to maintain unity of beliefs of His flock, is obvious and crystal clear! My reasoning has been influenced by prejudiced Christians who never bothered to consult the Catholic Church itself as to the reason *why* it teaches the beliefs that it does.

"Perhaps this is where the fault lies...in the Bible alone doctrine instead of referring to Sacred Tradition to support the Holy Scriptures for correct interpretation. The importance of Sacred Tradition as early as the second century seems to have been ignored! It is clear to me now why interpretations and translations of God's Word have been left to the authority of the Catholic Church to keep it unified. Perhaps Bible verses have been privately interpreted and quoted out-of-context, and in fact...those few verses are quoted repeatedly and stressed to evangelical Christians until they become second nature to them. I concur that Clement, whose letters were regarded as scripture, was stressing the importance of good works in the 1st century, and it is obvious that it was not *faith alone* that saved the early Christians, nor were they given assurance of their salvation! Purgatory and the perpetual virginity of Mary are additional beliefs that I can now better comprehend. Never did I bother to inspect simple, unbiased sources such as encyclopedias, that were as near as the public library. I will attempt to make right any injustice I have shown to Catholics in the past and to every Catholic I shall encounter in the future. I can now discern that even further instruction is needed.

"First, I will aspire to educate my congregation on all knowledge I have gained herewith. Then, when all is made right once again, I will consider entrance into the Church founded by Jesus Christ almost 2,000 years ago, a Church which heresy and schisms have repeatedly tried to destroy but has withstood the test of time, uncompromising in her beliefs and moral values. The true meaning and value of Apostolic Succession was never made known to me, but it truly is a notable treasure of the Church. I bid you farewell and thank you once again for this heavenly journey to the early Church."

With a glorious heavenly smile, Gabriel nodded his approval, extended his magnificent wings and at once, Carter found himself once again in his bedroom.

* * * * *

It was as if time had stood motionless, for upon his arrival, it was still the middle of the night, and his garments had once again returned to his normal nightly attire.

Slipping into his comfortable bed, Carter laid his head gently on his pillow and softly and meaningfully prayed the *Lord's Prayer*. However, this time...it seemed to have an entirely new meaning! This time, the prayer was not for his human needs, nor was it a request for food upon his table. Now, the prayer seemed new, almost pristine...for it was the prayerful request for two of Carter's essential requirements for his eternal salvation: the provision of God's heavenly bread, the Eucharist, and the forgiveness of all of his sins.

"Amen...So be it," he said as he closed his eyes.

THE END

BIBLIOGRAPHY

REFERENCES

Encyclopedia Britannica, Inc., 23 Volumes, William Benton, Chicago, Illinois, 1966.

The Encyclopedia Americana, International Edition, 30 Volumes, Grolier Inc., Danbury, Connecticut 1991.

The Encyclopedia of Early Christianity, Everett Ferguson, Garland Publishing, Inc., New York and London, 1990.

Holy Bible, Revised Standard Version, Second Edition, Thomas Nelson, Inc., Nashville, Tennessee, 1971.

Holy Bible, Authorized King James Version, School and Library Reference 1965-66 Edition, The John A. Hertel Co., Chicago, Illinois, 1963.

The Holy Bible, Douay-Rheims Version, Translated from the Latin Vulgate, TAN Books and Publishers, Inc., Rockford, Illinois 61105, 1971.

The Interpreter's Bible, VII, Abingdon Press, Nashville, Tennessee, 1987.

The New American Bible, Thomas Nelson Publishers, Nashville, Tennessee, 1979.

The New Jerusalem Bible, Doubleday, New York, New York, 10103, 1985.

1992 Catholic Almanac, Felician A. Foy, O.F.M. and Rose M. Avato, Our Sunday Visitor Publishing Division, Huntington, Indiana.